ANGELS
OF
LOVE

ALSO BY GRANT VIRTUE

Angel Words (with Doreen Virtue; book)

Angels of Abundance (with Doreen Virtue; book)

Angel Blessings Candle Kit (with Doreen Virtue; includes booklet, CD, journal, etc.)

ALSO BY MELISSA VIRTUE

Angel Dreams (with Doreen Virtue; book)

Angel Dreams Oracle Cards (with Doreen Virtue; card deck)

All of the above are available at your local bookstore, or may be ordered by visiting:

Hay House USA: www.hayhouse.com®
Hay House Australia: www.hayhouse.com.au
Hay House UK: www.hayhouse.co.uk
Hay House South Africa: www.hayhouse.co.za
Hay House India: www.hayhouseco.in

Grant's website: www.GrantVirtue.com
Melissa's website: www.SacredSolas.com

ANGELS OF LOVE

5 Heaven-Sent Steps to Find and Keep the Perfect Relationship

GRANT VIRTUE AND MELISSA VIRTUE

HAY HOUSE, INC.
Carlsbad, California • New York City
London • Sydney • Johannesburg
Vancouver • New Delhi

Published and distributed in the United States by: Hay House, Inc.: www.hayhouse
.com® • *Published and distributed in Australia by:* Hay House Australia Pty. Ltd.: www.
hayhouse.com.au • *Published and distributed in the United Kingdom by:* Hay House
UK, Ltd.: www.hayhouse.co.uk • *Published and distributed in the Republic of South
Africa by:* Hay House SA (Pty), Ltd.: www.hayhouse.co.za • *Distributed in Canada by:*
Raincoast Books: www.raincoast.com • *Published in India by:* Hay House Publishers India:
www.hayhouse.co.in

Cover design: Charles McStravick • *Interior design:* Nick C Welch

A previous edition of this book was published by VirtuePress.org (ISBN: 978-0-6155-8375-4)

Library of Congress Cataloging-in-Publication Data

Names: Virtue, Grant, author. | Virtue, Melissa, author.
Title: Angels of love : 5 heaven-sent steps to find and keep the perfect relationship / Grant Virtue
and Melissa Virtue. Description: Carlsbad, California : Hay House, [2017]
Identifiers: LCCN 2016037601| ISBN 9781401951597 (tradepaper : alk. paper) |
  ISBN 9780615583754
Subjects: LCSH: Love--Miscellanea. | Mate selection--Miscellanea. |
  Interpersonal relations--Miscellanea. | Spiritual life.
Classification: LCC BF1999 .V59 2017 | DDC 131--dc23 LC record available at https://lccn.loc.
gov/2016037601

Tradepaper ISBN: 978-1-4019-5159-7

10 9 8 7 6 5 4 3 2 1
1st Hay House edition, January 2017

Printed in the United States of America

To Melissa, my angel of love
— GV

To the Angels of Love, who reunited
me with my soul mate, Grant
— MV

CONTENTS

FOREWORD

God and the angels *are* pure love and, in spiritual truth, so are you. At some level, you remember the sweet and unconditional love that you felt in Heaven, prior to your birth. In Heaven, you felt respected, loved, and understood . . . and you're seeking this same experience in your earthly relationships.

If you're craving love and companionship, it's important to tread carefully in your quest. After all, those who feel lonely often settle for unsuitable relationships because they want to fill a void. God and the angels don't want you to settle because they know that you'll still feel lonely and unhappy within an unsuitable relationship.

In *The Angels of Love*, Grant and Melissa Virtue offer practical guidance to help you create a relationship that mirrors your memories of Heaven's love. Their empowering approach to healthy romantic love teaches how to stay true to yourself in a partnership.

Grant and Melissa not only write about healthy love but also live it! I've watched them navigate through stressful situations as a unified couple, without any of the negative habits such as blaming or distancing which can erode the experience of love. They walk their talk as a couple, and show that healthy relationships are fun, passionate, and purposeful.

As you read this book, my prayer is that you'll be inspired and remain optimistic about all of your relationships. After all, everything that you learn about healthy romantic relationship dynamics, such as respect, honesty, and communication, is applicable to friendships and families.

May you feel the love that Heaven is sending to you continuously and enjoy healthy, respectful, joyous relationships.

With Love,

Doreen

INTRODUCTION

Partnering with the Angels of Love

This book was written for anyone who's currently seeking the perfect relationship. However, finding the ideal life partner is only half the story. Once you actually *have* a wonderful relationship, it's important to take definitive steps to keep it.

Relationships at every level are spiritual endeavors, as it is the Divine spark within you that seeks to come together with others for mutual enjoyment. This level of joy takes many forms depending on the type of relationship you're involved in. Business relationships are formed with the mutual financial success of all parties in mind; social clubs are started so that their members can feel as if they're part of something (and sometimes to help those in need). And even street gangs are a type of relationship that is created to protect the members.

Romantic relationships are formed for all the above reasons but with one unique and important difference: *the coming together of two people for a lifelong partnership is primarily based on love.* While it's possible for other types of relationships, such as business- and social-based relationships, to eventually include a form of love, it's rarely the primary reason for the partnership.

Love is a very tricky thing to define, as it cannot be measured by any known method. No one can tell someone else whether he or she feels love at any given moment or feels it about anyone in particular. It is at once the most *personal* and the most *interpersonal* feeling we humans are capable of. Nor is love limited to occurring among human beings only. The love felt for an animal is similar in many ways to that which is felt for another person.

In this book, we'll discuss why love is such a critical emotion in our lives, as well as how true love can be attained. We won't encourage you to stay with someone simply because that person is easy to be with, or to settle for the first partner who comes your way. This book is about finding and keeping true and everlasting love.

No one person is more qualified than another to obtain true love. We all have it within ourselves to seek out and connect with that perfect partner whom we can be in a relationship with. Perhaps you've heard that some people are lucky in life and others are lucky in love. It's our assertion that this is one and the same thing. Someone who's wise and introspective enough to decide whether someone is the right person—or just the person who happens to be there right now—is also an individual who can generate his or her own luck.

Perhaps you feel that you're currently in the perfect relationship, and you're reading this book to help out a friend or loved one. This is a just and noble cause, and we salute you for it. However, when reading these words, please be aware of those areas of your *own* love life that could be improved upon. And please know that we're not advocating leaving your current partner for someone new—it would be much better for both of you if the relationship you're currently in would transform into one of mutual love, respect, devotion, and happiness.

Our Spiritual Perspectives

Melissa: Connecting and communicating with Source and the angels plays a vital role in my life. I've had a relationship with the angels since I was a young girl. Although I grew up in a home where we went to church on Sundays, the angels weren't discussed. However, I would receive messages from the angels during my nightly dreams, which was the beginning of my journey in dream interpretation.

A week after graduating from college, I moved to New York City, where I pursued a professional dance career. Throughout my career I continued working with the angels and my guides. They led me toward the study of many healing modalities and the continuance of dream interpretation.

Dance, for me, is a sacred, spiritual art form. We can be connected with Source, love, and the universe through sacred movement, and I wanted to share this with others in a way that wasn't technical or competitive. I wanted *everyone* to be able to connect movement with spirit. Therefore, after I left the professional dance world, I was guided to create a form of spiritual dance. At this time I also began receiving clients for various healing modalities, including dream interpretation and intuitive readings, which I have been doing worldwide for over 20 years now. I give thanks to Source and the angels for continuing learning and guidance.

Grant: I grew up in a household where working with angels was a matter of course. It was stressed from an early age that any issues or desires that I had could be handled by asking my angels for help. Growing up in such a way made connecting with my angels as an adult feel very natural and safe.

Throughout my youth and into my adult years, I accompanied my mother, Doreen Virtue, on many of her domestic and international tours. I was privileged to meet and speak with hundreds of people from all over the world, as well as listen to several incredibly talented and knowledgeable spiritual teachers. Through these myriad lessons and encounters, I realized what a profound opportunity for healing the angels provided.

I have since gone on to study a variety of topics, ranging from health to psychology to law. In each of these disciplines, I have utilized the gifts of the angels to assist both myself and others. I have found that any situation, any subject—indeed, any aspect of my life—can be improved by calling upon God and my angels for help and guidance.

Who Are the Angels of Love?

The Angels of Love are a council of angels who help each person find their ideal soul-mate relationship. Not only do they help us *find* our perfect life partner but they help us *maintain* a healthy, loving relationship. The Angels of Love offer guidance, support, tools, and techniques, as well as help us problem-solve issues, so we may keep our wonderful intimate relationships intact.

The concepts in this book are a compilation of what we both learned over the years from the Angels of Love. We have tested and tried each one of them. In fact, these concepts are what finally led us to each other!

Melissa's Angels of Love Story

The Angels of Love first introduced themselves to me when I was living in New York City. While the dance technique I studied was teaching me nonverbal communication, via body language and the psychology of a man's or woman's inner landscape, the Angels of Love were sending me lessons in how to truly trust in a partnership and how to take honest steps no matter how vulnerable I felt. They gave me lessons through my own relationship choices, as well as those of family and friends. With this knowledge, combined with my formal training, I began to understand how healthy romantic relationships truly function. Of course, I still didn't fully recognize the purpose of the Angels of Love until I encountered them again many years later.

This time, these angelic beings appeared in my dreams, showing me how to release the unhealthy relationship in which I was entangled. In one dream, they revealed to me that there was another path I could choose, one where my soul mate was waiting for me. At the time, I couldn't make out the details of what my "dream" partner looked like, but I did meet him and had the opportunity to feel his amazing presence.

Upon awakening, I knew I was being guided and supported in the soul-mate department. This dream helped me recognize how much I yearned for my soul mate and a loving relationship. Fortunately, the Angels of Love showed me it was not too late to find a wonderful man I could choose to love.

After this dream, I began recognizing the guidance from the Angels of Love, whether I was dreaming or awake. I built a relationship with them by trusting their loving, supportive messages. The Angels of Love not only showed me the steps to

take but taught me the tools and techniques I needed to apply in order to bring my soul mate into my life.

A year later, I met my true love, Grant.

Grant's Angels of Love Story

Like Melissa, the Angels of Love revealed themselves to me slowly over a number of years. I had been in previous relationships that, while significant at the time, were absurdly one-sided. This pattern occurred so often and continued for so long that I had come to the conclusion that this was just the way relationships were meant to work. I also wondered if perhaps something was wrong with me because I felt unfulfilled.

However, I started to receive very clear and loving guidance that relationships did not have to follow this particular track. I began noticing other couples who had more satisfying relationships and knew that these people were being presented to me by the Angels of Love as examples.

Once I met Melissa, the messages I had been receiving for the previous few years suddenly made sense. If I had not heard from the Angels of Love, I probably would have felt undeserving of the positive experiences I was sharing with her. Nevertheless, I had been taught some important lessons and realized that the relationship we were cultivating was not something unusual, but a model of how a soul-mate relationship is *supposed* to be!

Over the years, Melissa and I have gathered information on relationship health and communication through formal study, observations, life lessons, and the teachings from the Angels of Love.

Working with the Angels of Love

The Angels of Love are somewhat different from the Romance Angels you may have read or heard about previously. Their goals are similar, but the *scope* of their goals is very different. Rather than being focused on the immediate here and now, the Angels of Love are more concerned with making sure that your relationship promotes your greatest long-term good.

This is not to say that there shouldn't be romance in your relationship! On the contrary, the Angels of Love know that romance is an integral part of keeping any relationship alive and healthy. However, it's entirely possible to have a romantic relationship with someone who's all wrong for you. In fact, some of the most romantic relationships of all time were completely dysfunctional. As such, the Angels of Love want to make sure that yours is both passionate *and* fulfilling. They help you go beyond the surface of romantic love so you may delve deeper into the profound levels of soul-mate love.

Working with the angels is the easy part of this book. They are Divine beings who possess eternal love and patience, and offer unconditional support. You can never request something from them that they will not lovingly and thoroughly consider. You can be sure that every time you invoke their holy names, you are surrounded by loving beings who desire only the very best for you. When you put your trust in these beings of love and light, you can do so knowing that they're looking after you in all ways and that you have nothing to fear.

The Angels of Love imparted their messages to us through thoughts, visions, and emotions. When you work with these powerful beings, you may notice that they will also start giving you messages in a variety of ways. One of the main methods we used to gather information from the Angels of Love was to meditate on the specific question we wanted to know about, and then listen for them to give us the answer. So many times when writing, we felt as if the angels were virtually controlling our hands and typing out precisely what they felt humanity needed to know the most.

How to Use This Book

This book is intended to be a workbook of sorts. Steps 3 and 4, in particular, are meant to be read over again whenever you need them. We've attempted to be as inclusive as possible, while ensuring that the information is approachable even for absolute beginners to spirituality and working with angels.

Throughout the process of writing this book, we asked for and received stories from people who were able to make a love connection with the help of God and the Angels of Love. We have included these inspirational stories in several chapters to show how communicating with the Angels of Love can have powerful effects on your life.

If you use this book in the manner in which it's intended, regardless of your prior experiences, you'll dramatically improve the odds of finding the right person. However, it *does* require work on your part and more than a little faith that God and the angels are simultaneously working on your behalf. Faith requires that you're comfortable with what you're doing. If anything you try—including a step in this book—makes you feel uncomfortable, stop doing it.

— The most important task ahead of you is to define exactly what you want in a partner (**Step 1**). You may already have someone in mind whom you believe to be perfect for you. That's fine, as long as you don't close yourself off to other people. We are sometimes blinded by our preferences and can spend too much time focusing on someone who will never be right for us.

— The Angels of Love will help you find that ideal mate, but they can do so only if you stay out of your own way. So, you'll need to take steps to help heal yourself from past hurts and betrayals (**Step 2**) so that you don't inadvertently become a source of pain to your new mate. This isn't meant to be harsh, but simply honest. Just as you don't want to be with a partner riddled with issues, the other person also desires someone with enough stability to communicate without, for example, spontaneously bursting into tears or erupting in anger. You will certainly want to be able to fully focus on and enjoy your relationship without past issues horning in on your journey together.

— Once you've figured out exactly what you'd like in a partner, the angels will help you work on attracting that person (**Step 3**). Of course, this doesn't strictly apply to physical attraction. We're referring to attracting someone on a physical, energetic, *and* spiritual level. The Angels of Love will remove the blocks you've put up that bar love from entering your life. Nothing will stand between you and the perfect relationship that you've always wanted, needed, and deserved.

Trust that the angels will match you with someone who will fulfill you more than you can imagine. You don't need to fear that this new partner will be *less than* the person you happen to have in mind. If, on the other hand, the man or woman you do have in mind *is* the right person for you, then you can trust that the angels will arrange for the two of you to get together. In either case, you simply need to trust and let go.

— With that said, there are still some tasks you must work on yourself (**Step 4**). God and the Angels of Love do want you to have the best mate imaginable, but you'll have to meet them halfway to make this a reality. You'll need to use your discernment to find out if this man or woman is as perfect as you believe in your new-relationship-induced state of bliss . . . or if this is just someone who happens to be giving you attention.

— A special note if you are currently in a relationship: As we touched upon previously, this book will definitely help you, too. Your relationship can be made better, and you can find the fulfillment you desire with the man or woman you're already with (**Step 5**). But if, after a long and thoughtful process, you decide that it's time to move on, this book will help you find new love and recover from your past hurts.

— You will also benefit from keeping a journal or notebook near you for notes, as well as for the various writing and meditation exercises contained within this book. The meditations at the back (**Appendix**) can be used to help clear your mind of distracting thoughts so you focus on exactly whom you are trying to manifest.

Thank you for joining us on this adventure. Now let's get to work!

DEFINE YOUR PERFECT RELATIONSHIP

Identifying and Affirming What You Want in a Partner

God and the Angels of Love have a very strong desire to see you in the perfect relationship. So much of the guidance you—and all of us—receive throughout life is geared toward a loving and fulfilling partnership. The Angels of Love are happy to help you reach this goal, but they will need some assistance from *you*. In order for them to bring you the perfect relationship, you have to know what that *means* to you.

When we discuss the perfect relationship, we must be very clear that it is the *relationship* that we desire to be perfect, not the person we're with. Each of us, for better or worse, comes with built-in flaws and idiosyncrasies that make us unique. We must be understanding and forgiving of other people's flaws and foibles, just as we would like others to be forgiving and understanding of our own. We must never get to the point where we're so particular that we can't tolerate even the slightest personality quirks in others.

The perfect relationship means something different to everyone. For some people, it is one in which you wake up and fall asleep madly in love with the person next to you. For others, it may simply mean being with someone who lets you be yourself. Still others are in search of someone who shares every interest and activity and who is a faithful and constant companion.

For the rest of the steps in this book to be effective for you, you will have to come up with your own personal definition of the perfect relationship. Every aspect must be covered, but know that you won't be alone in this search. You will always have the Angels of Love to call upon to help you.

We will start this very important process by saying a prayer together:

God, please send Your Angels of Love to me now. I desire a partner so that I may continue with my life purpose without the burden of loneliness.

Angels of Love, please come to me now and guide me in finding the perfect relationship. Look into my heart and help me define precisely what I need in a partner and partnership.

I am open to all the Divine support and intervention necessary to help me achieve this goal of being in an ideal relationship. I accept only goodness and kindness from my potential life partner, and I give only goodness and kindness in return.

God, You Who are the Divine master of love itself, please keep me safe while I open myself up to love. Please see to it that only loving people are sent my way, and please redirect those who belong on a path different from mine.

Thank You, God. Thank you, angels. I joyfully enter into this search with you now.

The preceding prayer is not, strictly speaking, necessary to initiate this process, but it will certainly help. It is vitally important to remember that Divine forces are looking out for you, you're not alone in this undertaking, and you don't need to fend for yourself. By keeping in regular contact with your Divine Creator through prayer, you will be much happier during your search and will have a much easier time of it.

Write It Down

Now that you've called upon your Divine reinforcements, it's time to get down to the business of figuring out exactly what you want to manifest. For this exercise, you'll need pen and paper.

1. Write down 11 of the traits you'd like to see in your partner. Eleven is a very significant angel number. It is considered a master number, representing the combining of the powerful male energy with the equally potent female energy. Choosing to write 11 qualities adds that extra charge of energy to your manifestation. You don't need to list them in any particular order. Just jot down the first things that pop into your head. For example, do you want your partner to be kind? Beautiful?

Rich? Outgoing? Generous? Write down any sort of attributes you want your new or existing partner to possess.

2. Once you've listed those traits, use a new piece of paper to describe the circumstances you see yourself involved in with this person. Think about what you want the relationship to look like: Are you married? Or is it a civil union? Do you have kids, a dog, and a house with a yard? Is your relationship based on a mutual love of Harley motorcycles? Of tennis? This part of the exercise is meant to encourage you to think of every aspect of your partnership. You don't want to find the perfect person only to discover that he or she wants something entirely different from what you want.

Although you must be very clear from the beginning as to what type of relationship you're interested in, you may, of course, change your mind at a future point. If you start this exercise with no interest in marriage but later decide that getting married isn't such a bad idea after all, this could be a potential problem if your partner isn't on the same page. However, if you act with a small amount of foresight now, you can prevent this sort of dilemma from arising. You simply need to ensure that the partner you're trying to attract is flexible.

You've now written down a few very specific personality traits on one piece of paper, and a reasonable description of the exact type of relationship you desire on another. As simple as it may seem, this is a very good start. The majority of relationships are made or broken based on conflicting personality traits and the pursuit of different life goals.

It would be quite easy to fill a third piece of paper with personality traits you absolutely would *not* accept in a new partner. However, we encourage you to focus only on what you would like to *attract,* rather than what you would like to avoid. Maintaining a positive mind-set throughout this exercise—and indeed throughout your entire life—will bring you much more success in your manifestations. (*Manifestations* are goals that you accomplish with Divine help. These goals can come in the form of objects you desire, money, or a soul mate.)

Negative words, thoughts, and emotions carry very little energy in comparison to positivity. This doesn't necessarily mean that they're harmful, but rather that they're more or less useless. When you try to manifest with negativity in your mind, you cannot channel the required amount of energy to ensure that your work is paying off.

Conversely, positive words, thoughts, and emotions carry an enormous amount of energy, which directly translates into powerful manifestations. This has a lot to do with the fact that God and the angels do not want you to carry around negativity, and they will actively work against any attempt to manifest it. When you work with positivity, on the other hand, you're working in concert with Heaven and will be aided by this harmonious connection. (You can find more information about this topic in my [Grant's] first book, *Angel Words*.)

We understand that sometimes negative situations come up. If you let them, they can adversely affect your mood, thoughts, and emotions. We're not saying that you shouldn't express how you truly feel, but that you should avoid any and all negative manifestations during this time.

If you're already with someone and are hoping that this person will become the one you have a lifelong relationship with, the exercise is largely the same. You will, of course, have much less flexibility than a person who is seeking someone new. When you're dealing with a current relationship, you have to take the other person's right to free will into consideration and accept that you may not be able to transform every current trait into something that pleases you. After all, true love is unconditional.

Take those pieces of paper and set them aside for now, but periodically review the information and feel free to update it from time to time. The more precise your specifications are, the more accurate your manifestations will be. Your options are nearly limitless when it comes to human personalities, looks, and values, so the more specific you can be, the better.

Desiring and Aspiring vs. Pickiness

There's nothing wrong with setting requirements for the person you want to attract. Certainly it would be unfair to expect someone to conform to your every desire if you're already together. But, fortunately, that restriction doesn't apply to someone you haven't met yet. Right now, before you're paired with your partner, is the time to be highly choosy. Once you're with this person, you will want to revert to your normal, accepting self.

Forgiveness is also a very important part of this process. You may ask, "Why would I need to ever forgive this person if he or she is perfect for me?" Well, just because someone is perfect *for* you doesn't mean the individual in question is perfect. He or she will make mistakes just as often as you do and will need forgiveness just as you do. Obviously you won't want to be matched with someone who strays or is abusive—these are serious behavioral problems that must be avoided. However, normal, minor human errors are bound to show up even in the most dashing prince or beautiful princess.

You may wonder what the difference is between desiring and manifesting the perfect relationship and just being picky. In truth, they're miles apart. Desiring a perfect relationship means that you want someone who complements *you* in the same way you do him or her. A perfect relationship is a life in sync with your highest good, guided by God and the angels. Being picky, on the other hand, is merely a form of control. Nobody in a perfect relationship has any control over the other person; rather, the two parties work together quite naturally for their mutual betterment.

Affirmations Attract

Affirmations are another very useful tool that can help you attract the perfect relationship. Like prayer, affirmations are a way of vocalizing your desires so that the Angels of Love are free to help you. God and the angels would love to assist you with every issue in your life, but since you've been gifted with free will, they can intervene only when you ask them to. Affirmations are a way of continually asking for help so that you're never without Divine guidance.

Affirmations are essentially positive words, thoughts, and phrases that you repeat to yourself. You speak these affirmations in the present tense so that you know you're not waiting for a mythical future. By saying that you have these items or situations in your life *now* rather than later, you can plan for their eventuality. If you absolutely must speak of things in the future tense, use a finite period of time, such as "next week" or "14 days from now," rather than "soon" or, worse, "someday."

You can even use affirmations as a way of discerning the exact traits you desire in a perfect relationship. In other words, if you're manifesting a relationship, why not manifest clarity with respect to your desires? You're limitless in your ability to attract what you want into your life.

Digital Love

Robert of Calgary, Alberta, was a computer programmer for many years and had a very hard time finding the time and motivation to go out and meet women. Those he'd met in the past seemed more interested in having a male house servant than an equal partner. About the time Robert had essentially accepted that he would be alone for the rest of his life, he decided to try to manifest the love of his life, simply as an experiment. He figured he had nothing to lose.

Over the course of three months, Robert followed a dedicated schedule of praying for his future wife to come to him and affirming that he was in a loving, mutually respectful relationship. At first he didn't go out much, as he was still in a state of skepticism. However, he forced himself to start going to conventions and coffee shops to see the experiment through to the end.

One day he was sitting at a coffee shop reading a computer magazine when a woman came up to him. Robert was a bit hesitant because only very aggressive women had approached him previously. However, he felt a very strong pull toward this woman and took it as Divine guidance, so he didn't shy away. The woman turned out to be the author of the main article in the magazine and had noticed that Robert was reading it. Because he seemed particularly engrossed in the article—the first she'd ever written for a computer magazine—she wanted to get his opinion of it.

He told her how much he'd enjoyed reading the article, and they struck up a conversation. This was followed by several dates, and now they're happily engaged.

Robert reports that he's learned a great deal about the world *outside* of computers, and his fiancée has learned quite a bit *about* computers. Both of them feel that they're much better off in every aspect of their lives now that they've found each other. Robert directly attributes meeting his partner to the Angels of Love, who finally motivated him to get out there and find the kind of relationship he was looking for.

Robert's story illustrates how people need only a passing knowledge of basic spirituality to achieve remarkable results. Robert had learned about prayer and affirmations in a book he'd read 10 years prior. While practice *does* make perfect, and spiritual awareness ultimately leads to a blessed life, even absolute beginners can improve their situation with the help of these tools. Robert's story reminds us that no one is more or less connected to, or loved by, God and the angels.

~

The next section of this chapter will focus on how *you* can use the powerful tools of manifestation to improve yourself. Even if you feel that no area of your personal life could use a little adjusting, it's worth experimenting. You will want to be prepared for someone else to live with you and your habits. After all, a perfect relationship has *two* people in it, not just one.

Step into the Flow

Affirmations can be as simple or as complex as you want them to be. It doesn't necessarily follow that complex problems require complex affirmations. Often, the simpler you keep things, the easier they are to manage. For the purposes of this chapter, we're going to keep the affirmations as simple as possible. Your goal is to define the perfect relationship, primarily focusing on the specific traits you want in a partner.

Try to repeat the following affirmation as many times as possible. Some people feel that the repetition of affirmations can be used as a type of mantra that will help you establish a more open mind-set. Nevertheless, if you're satisfied with just saying it once, that is acceptable, provided that you really open yourself up to it. If you feel hesitant or find that your mind is wandering while you're reading and saying the affirmation, you may want to go over it again until it's no longer a challenge for you.

This affirmation will help you discharge any residual guilt or negative feelings about yourself that may be blocking your love life:

I deserve happiness in all ways. I am a worthy partner who is strong in my relationships. I accept only loving people, thoughts, and energy in my life. I have the perfect relationship now and will continue to have the perfect relationship for all time.

My relationship balances and inspires me. Only good comes from this relationship. As a team, we're working toward completing our life purpose with mutually loving support.

As you can see, this affirmation is not overly long and doesn't involve situations unrelated to your desire for the perfect relationship. The use of finite statements spoken in the present tense ensures that you're not going after some nebulous goal set in the distant future. These things are happening *now*, even as you read this. The universe is constantly in motion, and you are stepping into that flow.

Alleviate Fears and Worry

Once you've stated this simple affirmation and have let it start to work its magic, journal the thoughts and emotions it brings up for you. If you felt just fine throughout the whole process—great! Otherwise, try to express any worries that emerged. No matter what you are working on manifesting, the fear of success can interfere with your manifestations, so it's best to deal with those fears as they arise.

If you are concerned that having a perfect relationship will change your life purpose—or bring *any* unwelcome changes to your life—you can ask the Angels of Love to help you release that fear. For example, you may be afraid that if you manifest this relationship, you will lose friends, or your life will change dramatically in ways you aren't prepared for. Although manifesting your desires brings many changes to your life, these are for your highest good. They will be *wonderful* changes! Remember, in regard to your life purpose, you're given specific gifts in order to achieve success. Having the perfect relationship will not take away from, but only lend more support to, your life purpose and encourage you to continue along its path.

If you *do* find that the fear of success is interfering with your manifestation work, there are many ways to alleviate this fear:

First, remember that what you are manifesting will work out for the greater good of everyone.

Second, remember that everyone experiences the fear of success from time to time. You're not alone, and this doesn't mean that you're somehow unworthy of having that desired loving relationship. The only thing you need to focus on is removing external distractions that are keeping you from progressing on your path. For example, you may feel your financial situation is holding you back. Perhaps you even feel that due to your financial status you don't deserve a relationship. That's why the Angels of Love, as well as the Angels of Abundance, want you to ask them for help.

(The Angels of Abundance are closely related to the Angels of Love, as they are both assigned to us to help us remove the barriers to achieving our life purpose. In the case of the Angels of Abundance, as I [Grant] discuss in the book of the same name, co-authored with my mother, Doreen, the barriers they are re-leasing are largely financial but can also encompass other areas of your life that require more abundance. They know that the more obstacles they remove from your life, the more likely you are to fulfill your mission.)

Get Clarity in Dream Time

If you aren't certain what fears may be blocking you from having the perfect relationship, you can ask the Angels of Love to bring you clear guidance during your dream time. That's right! Your dreams are messages from the Divine. As I (Melissa) discuss in the book *Angel Dreams* (co-authored with Doreen), they are important tools for your growth.

You can ask the Angels of Love to give you insight during your dreams. When you sleep, your conscious mind gets out of the way, thereby allowing the Angels of Love, among other Divine messengers, to bring important information to you. Before sleeping, call upon the Angels of Love and ask them to reveal any fears that may be keeping your soul mate at bay. In dream time, the Angels of Love will bring you the answers you need to know. When you awaken in the morning, journal the message you received in your dreams. You will definitely begin to understand and see clearly what may be blocking your path. Then you can use powerful affirmations to combat and release these fears.

Customize Your Affirmations

Also, know that you're not limited to the one affirmation given above. You're free to create your own affirmations, which you can tailor to the specific type of relationship you have in mind. Once you've completed the steps delineated earlier in this chapter, you will most likely have a better idea of the type of person and relationship you're trying to manifest. When that occurs, making another affirmation will be quite easy for you. You will simply state in a believable and confident manner that you have this type of relationship *now*. Positive words stated confidently and strongly have a remarkable power to effect change in your life.

Now that you've completed the exercises in this chapter, you should have a fairly good handle on your personal definition of the perfect relationship. Once again, we must emphasize that this definition should be subject to change over time. You're constantly maturing and evolving, so your definition should also mature and evolve. If you went purely on the criteria you might have chosen when you were younger, your current self would find the resulting relationship unsatisfying.

Keep the lists and other notes you made while you worked on this chapter, as you will be adding to them in subsequent chapters. These lists will also be used in several manifestation exercises later on. If you ever decide that they no longer serve you, feel free to write new ones at any point.

Here You Go!

Congratulations! You've taken the first step to manifesting the perfect relationship. Often the first step is the hardest, and this was a rather large leap forward on your path. We will be forging ahead in the next chapter, so be sure to take a rest—you've certainly earned it!

STEP 2

RELEASE WHAT'S HOLDING YOU BACK

Out with the Old

God and the angels love you exactly the way you are and know that you are a Divine and perfect being. People, though, are not always quite so understanding and wise.

Each of us has gotten where we are today due to any number of external circumstances, most of which are beyond our control. The end result is that the majority of us are really great people, but we have a few areas of our lives that need to be fine-tuned a bit. In a few cases, the fine-tuning required is more of a full overhaul.

This chapter is about getting rid of those things in your life that no longer serve you—anything from habits and quirks . . . to possessions, exes, or even geographical locations. Only *you* know what is holding you back; no one can decide that for you. All that matters is releasing those things and issues—forever. You want to clear yourself of any residue that might block your progress toward your aspirations. This residue can be like spiderwebs, sticky and messy, spreading over everything. Therefore you need to begin with a clean slate, sweeping away the vestiges of anything unwanted. This allows you to create and attract that which you desire in your life, including your perfect relationship.

With the help of God and the Angels of Love, you will ensure that those old issues never come back to haunt you— they've served their purpose. Obviously not everything you need to let go of is necessarily bad. We aren't making judgment calls on whether these things should exist in the first place or should somehow be other than what they are. We're concerned only with eradicating them from your life so you can move on and grow.

Releasement Techniques

So how do we go about removing these unwanted and unwelcome influences? We start by asking for help. As stated previously, we're both gifted and burdened with free will. We can easily rid ourselves of the burdensome aspect of this gift by asking for Divine intervention whenever we need it. By giving God permission to intervene on our behalf, we receive the best of both worlds: self-rule and benevolent guidance.

There are several ways you can ask for help. Each is effective, but different methods seem to work better for different people. Perhaps this is because some methods feel more comfortable than others when you're performing them. Or it could be that some methods help you concentrate on the task at hand more easily than others. For this reason, we advise that you try each of these methods and see which one you find most comfortable and effective. The true measure of a tool is how well it works for you. If something looks beautiful and attractive but fails for you every time, it's not a tool that you need to use any longer.

For the more technically minded, it's important to note that these practices aren't what would commonly be referred to as tools of *manifestation*. Rather, these techniques fall under the category of *releasement*. You may find that your releasement techniques vary in effectiveness depending on the time of day, phase of the moon, or season of the year. These things can strengthen or diminish the energy for releasement. Think about it like fuel for transportation. The more fuel (energy) a car has, the longer distance it can go to reach a particular destination (releasement). If there is not much fuel, the car peters out. Therefore, your intentions for releasement will go much further if the conditions are right and you're operating with a "full tank." This is the reason some pay attention to the time of day, phase of the moon, or season of year, so they make sure to choose "high-octane" times.

If you're one of those individuals who works with these effective energetic times, please time your work accordingly. You can use the Full Moon Releasement Ceremony that follows or create one of your own. Best times of day for releasement are twilight and sunset. End of autumn through winter are the most potent seasons for releasement. For beginners who just want to get on with the business of releasing past hurts, worries, and burdens, you're free to start anytime.

Full Moon Releasement Ceremony

You can perform this anytime during the full moon day or in the evening before bed. You can choose to be indoors or outside.

What you will need: A pencil, scraps of paper, a fireproof bowl or cooking pot, a small bowl of water, a candle, matches or a lighter, a sacred space (an area, large or small, where you will not be interrupted [including by phones]), and an altar or some sort of table.

Preparation: Declutter your space and drape your altar with a lovely fabric of your choice. Place sacred or personal items— such as fresh flowers, crystals (moonstone is best for attuning to the rhythmic energies of the moon), a potted plant, incense, music, and spiritual symbols—on your altar or in this space. Set both bowls on the table, along with the candle and matches.

1. *Sain* (bless) the space with prayer, music, and chimes, or by sprinkling water, smudging, or chanting *Om*.

2. Cleanse your energy by imagining a waterfall of silver light pouring over the crown of your head and down your body as it washes away all negative energies.

3. Light the candle.

4. Take a few deep breaths and call upon your spirit guide, angels, passed-over loved ones, ascended masters, or anyone of Divine Love and Light you want to help with your releasing ceremony.

5. On the scraps of paper, write down all you want to release, including limiting thoughts.

6. Connect to your heart space by taking a deep breath. Declare, "I now release _____ [read off one scrap of paper]. And so it is."

7. Light the scrap with the candle and place in the fireproof bowl.

8. Repeat Steps 6 and 7 for as many scraps of paper as you have written upon.

9. Place your hands in the bowl of water to cleanse the old and initiate the new. Give gratitude. You can also choose to sprinkle the water around your head and body with your fingers.

10. Sit in silence a few minutes while you breathe deeply. Extinguish the candle when you feel complete.

Prayer

While the ceremony above should be performed at the full moon, the first method to try is by far the easiest: *prayer*. We already did a brief invocation at the start of Step 1, but we want to emphasize that prayer means very different things to different people. For the purposes of this book, we ask that you pray in the manner that feels most comfortable for you. We will guide you through a sample releasement prayer; however, we encourage you to use it only if it resonates with you. Studies have shown that prayer is effective depending on the sincerity of the person praying. If you're not comfortable with a particular prayer, then you won't be able to be sincere about it.

You can pray in a large group or by yourself. Some people feel that prayers must be uttered aloud, whereas others believe they should be silent. There are those who are taught to utilize only a single prayer no matter what the circumstance, and others who feel the need to go into a detailed dialogue during their prayer. Regardless of how you pray, or even whom you pray to, you can take comfort in the fact that it works.

Prayer is by far the single most powerful tool at our disposal and, interestingly enough, the one that is showing the most signs of neglect in our society. This can in part be attributed to lower attendance of churches, which is the only place where most people believe they can pray. However, it is not necessary to be in a site of worship to have a spiritual experience—and it's the same for prayer. You can pray on your own, anywhere, anytime.

What makes prayer so powerful is that you are, in essence, engaging in a personal conversation with your Divine Creator. We all know that the best way to get what we want is to ask for it. Who better to ask than the Creator of all people and things? A cheeky fellow recently teased us about these beliefs by comparing this important teaching to the old Janis Joplin song

"Mercedes Benz," in which she petitions the Lord to buy her a luxury vehicle. While he and Ms. Joplin were likely poking fun, it does not diminish the reality of the situation.

Faith in the power of the Divine Creator leads to sincerity of prayer, which in turn leads to answered prayers. How, then, can a cynical person ever properly test the power of prayer? Doesn't the very act of doubting color the results?

Everyone is entitled to his or her own beliefs, but those who keep an open mind are generally happier and more successful. We are also not trying to push a particular religion on anyone. We believe that a person's faith is the most personal thing in the entire world. Placing one faith above all others is not the answer to happiness. On the other hand, faith—in any form—is one of the key components of true happiness.

A prayer to help you heal from your past hurts doesn't necessarily have to be all-inclusive in order to be effective. You don't have to confess any wrongs you've committed, unless you so desire. If you know what's holding you back, then it's a sure bet that God knows, too. You can trust that God will take care of what needs to be taken care of once you ask.

Even so, it can certainly be cathartic to lay it all out on the table. If you're burdened with guilt, sometimes speaking of your perceived wrongdoing can be exactly what you need to help clear your conscience. There's no reason to feel embarrassed if that's what you choose to do. Judgment, after all, is a wholly human creation.

A quick and simple prayer that is nonetheless very effective would look something like this:

> *God, please help me release all those things that are no longer serving me. I no longer wish to be burdened by my past; and I release all attachments to prior pain, guilt, and fear.*
>
> *Please separate me from whatever is trying to hold me back.*
>
> *Please help me experience only positive influences in my life from this moment on.*
>
> *Thank You for Your help now and for all time.*

You may notice that we didn't include any traditional closing commonly found in prayer. This is because these differ so widely depending on a practitioner's background. Feel free to add any valedictions such as "Amen," "So mote it be," or "And so it is"—or whatever you consider fitting and respectful. Only *you* can decide how best to pray for releasement.

Most people report a nearly instantaneous effect from a prayer such as the one above. You may feel lighter, happier, or perhaps just less burdened than before. Or you might get a peculiar sensation like butterflies in your stomach. This is viewed by some as definitive proof of the efficacy of prayer. If you don't feel anything of the sort, though, don't worry—the prayer is still working. Some people seem to experience these effects more than others, but this has nothing to do with the potency of prayers.

Contrary to popular belief, there's no such thing as an unanswered prayer. Every prayer, without exception, *is* answered. The answer may not be what you want it to be all the time, but that's only because granting that particular prayer would cause hardship for you later.

We're not dealing with a cold, unfeeling, and unthinking universe; rather, we are in a conversation with an infinite Source of wisdom. If a prayer is denied us, we must simply find the grace and wisdom to accept that it is for our highest good.

Forgiveness

Prayer *does* have a remarkable power to heal our lives and create positive change; however, it is not the only method available to us. Some people find prayer uncomfortable, and others prefer a more hands-on approach in life. That's understandable. After all, we were put here to initiate change on our own, so we may as well get on with it.

Our personal favorite of all the hands-on approaches is the act of forgiveness. We say *act* because it's an action that you have to take within yourself. A person doesn't "decide" to forgive someone, but actively *engages* in forgiving someone.

The first step to forgiveness is to come to peace with the term itself. Forgiveness doesn't mean that what someone did was okay. It doesn't mean that the person should be allowed to do it again or go unpunished by the proper authorities. And it certainly doesn't mean that you're obliged to have anything to do with that person unless you truly want to.

Forgiveness simply means that you're letting go of your anger toward this person. You're recognizing that each of us is a child in the eyes of God, and we're prone to making mistakes. It is, at the very core, a recognition that holding on to anger causes a great deal of harm to ourselves, but absolutely none to the person we're angry with. As I (Grant) stated in my earlier book *Living a Blessed Life*, forgiveness is the greatest gift you will ever give or receive.

Forgiveness is an exercise that helps free you from past hurts and burdens, much like prayer does. When you forgive someone, you're releasing all parts of your life connected with the person who may be holding you back. You are also releasing the blocks to your happiness that the unforgiveness caused.

We've known many people who held themselves back by clinging to anger that originated in the distant past. In some cases decades had gone by, but these individuals still blamed ex-partners, parents, or others for the failings in their lives. These people didn't believe that their lives could be any other way because of old issues that were still affecting them. If they'd only forgiven the people in question and moved on, they probably wouldn't have limited themselves in so many ways.

If you have any—and we really mean *any*—person in your life or your life history whom you haven't forgiven, it's critical to your journey to do so *now*. If you're still holding on to anger, hurt, pain, mistrust, or any other negative emotion from the past, you will have an exponentially harder time attracting a perfect relationship. Even if you decide to forgive others for "selfish" reasons, such as wanting to clear yourself spiritually and emotionally before you seek out a new relationship, that's perfectly fine. This is definitely a situation where the end justifies the means, so forgive by any means necessary.

Forgiveness can also help you stop yourself from reacting to a completely new situation following an old pattern. For example, if a certain look crossed your ex's face every time he or she was upset, you may find yourself reacting to a new partner who gives you a similar look that may mean something else entirely. When you forgive your ex, you free yourself to learn what your new partner's particular expressions mean. This also frees your new partner from having to deal with your misconceptions.

Forgiveness can go the other way as well. Often the very person you need to forgive is *yourself.* You can carry around a huge amount of blame that you've heaped on yourself. Perhaps you regret your actions at a particular juncture or don't feel that you're quite living life up to your full potential. Addicts and those in recovery are especially prone to self-blame. If this sounds like you, then you owe it to yourself to release the self-condemnation that you're holding on to.

You, like everyone else, are a Divine child of God and should be given the same leniency and love that you give to everyone else. By shedding any residual anger and blame, you allow yourself to grow as a human. You no longer limit yourself based on your fears and untrue beliefs.

Sincerity is as crucial to forgiveness as it is to prayer. There's no point in saying that you've forgiven someone, including yourself, if you keep holding on to resentment. No one keeps track of your progress except you. You know within yourself whether or not you're being honest in all things.

Prayer + Forgiveness = Healing

We encourage you to try the two effective techniques we've discussed here: prayer and forgiveness. Their combined power is enough to successfully alter anyone's life for the better. This chapter is all about ensuring that you've properly cleansed yourself from your past before moving on. We want you to build your new life on a very firm foundation. If you've been truly honest with yourself, are sincere in your prayers, and really strive to forgive, then you'll attain what you want. We can say this unequivocally, and it bears repeating: *You will reach your goal.*

You must give yourself time to heal, though. You didn't reach this point in your life overnight. You are the product of every minute of every day. If some of those minutes have been especially difficult, you owe it to yourself to stop the pain now. If you don't immediately feel that you've let go of every past hurt and failed relationship in your life by the time you finish this book, that is quite normal. Consistency is the key. You'll have to pray on a regular basis, with the assurance that God and the Angels of Love are constantly looking after you, and you'll always have to remind yourself to forgive. Once you get used to these practices, they'll be like second nature to you.

Through a minimum of work on your part, you can free yourself from your past and set the stage to bring the perfect relationship into your life. You now know and accept that this can be a gradual process, but one that is worth the wait. You don't have to finish this process to enter into a new relationship, but you must be careful not to stop working toward the goal of healing simply because you're now with someone else. You and your new partner will be better off for the rest of your lives as a result of every minute you spend working on bettering yourself.

The exercise below will help you cultivate forgiveness. First go through the meditation, then follow it with the writing exercise.

Meditation: Healing Pool of Light

Find a comfortable, quiet spot where you can sit or lie down without being disturbed. Focus on your inhalations and exhalations, allowing your breath to dance throughout your body. In your mind's eye, see before you a lush garden growing with vibrant, fragrant flowers.

In the middle of this sacred garden is a sparkling pool of water. Walking closer to the pool, you realize it's not water, but golden light. You notice a bench next to the pool. As you sit on the bench, you begin to feel a great presence around you. This presence begins to coalesce into form, and you see before you a council of angels radiating various hues of color. These are the Angels of Love. Feel their unconditional love and support for you.

The Angels of Love beckon you to enter into the Healing Pool of Light. Stepping into the golden light, you feel it bathing you in warmth, support, and love from the crown of your head to the soles of your feet. The light around you shifts, and you see images before you as you would on a movie screen. These images are of people you have not forgiven. Choose one person from these images. Take a moment to feel the Angels of Love supporting you. They want you to be happy and free of burden. When you are ready to forgive and release this person, inhale and exhale deeply, allowing the golden light to wash over you. Feel your heart expand with love and forgiveness. Repeat "I forgive you" in your mind a few times. Feel the hurt, betrayal, and distrust wash away. Sense yourself becoming lighter and brighter. Do this again with another person. And continue until you have gone through all the people on your light screen.

How wonderful it feels to release the burdens you have been carrying around blocking you from happiness. You know that by releasing these hurts, you are making way for true love to enter into your life.

Stepping out of the pool, you stand before the Angels of Love. They embrace you one by one. They remind you that you can come back anytime to the Healing Pool of Light. Know that the Angels of Love are always with you; call upon them as often as you need. They are ready and waiting to help you on this amazing journey of love.

Writing Exercise: Blessings of Love

- Take your journal and write the name of each person you saw in the meditation.

- Next to each name write: *I forgive you.*

- At the bottom of this list, write: *I now forgive and release these people. I send them blessings of love. I now give myself the gift of love through forgiveness.*

- Write three things you are grateful for in your life right now.

- Last, write: *My heart is awake and open to giving and receiving love. I love. I am loved. I am love.*

Release the Fear of Loneliness

If this was a particularly difficult chapter to get through, we understand. Working on yourself can be scary, making you feel both selfish and vulnerable. Or you may even think the entire thing is unnecessary, as you fear you're destined to be alone. But trust us—this isn't the case.

Rarely is a person actually meant to be alone for life, but in such cases, he or she knows it from birth and is generally accepting of it. If you've ever feared that this may be you, please give that fear away to God right now. The very act of fearing that this may be your fate is a good indication that it is *not*. Those special few who have come to Earth to complete their missions by themselves have chosen this life, and they don't regret it. These individuals are surrounded by loving friends and close companions and can generally be found in monasteries, nunneries, and other seats of religious study. The hermit who has completely isolated him- or herself generally doesn't do so for life and is sometimes the unfortunate victim of a mental illness rather than a spiritual destiny.

You can, of course, force your way into a life of solitude. Some people completely cut themselves off from other people or have a generally bad attitude that effectively keeps others away. All someone would have to do to achieve this goal is completely ignore this chapter, steadfastly refuse to invite God and the angels into his or her life for help, and never forgive a soul. This would be a very miserable life, all things considered.

This person would likely have a hard time even making casual friends, let alone a meaningful connection. It's ludicrous to believe that a person of sound mind could have such a goal. Just by reading this book, you've demonstrated *your* commitment to connection.

At no point will you be alone on your journey. You are always surrounded by God and the angels. They are a constant in your life. The special spirit of God is what gives you life. Likewise, the Angels of Love are with you on this very special quest. They're thrilled that you've chosen to start working toward the perfect relationship. They have a Divine and holy mission to ensure that you attain your goal of love with a wonderful partner.

You Are on Your Way!

Congratulations for getting this far. You're off to a remarkable start. And so we conclude the chapter with this prayer:

God, thank You for coming into my life and sending Your Angels of Love. I trust that You will help me unburden myself from all my past hurts and pain. I forgive everyone in my life who has ever caused me harm, either intentionally or unintentionally. I forgive myself for every time I have failed to live up to my potential.

I ask You to free me, as I have tried to free myself, from every tether that is holding me down. Please help me choose only good for myself from this point forward. I am patient with myself and never treat myself harshly.

I wish to continue this journey holding Your Divine hand. Please continue to guide me for all eternity.

INVITE WHAT YOU DESIRE INTO YOUR LIFE

In with the New

Know that you are blessed with some very powerful God-given resources. Primary among them are the Angels of Love. Acting as God's messengers, they will help you every step of the way as you go about attracting your life partner. There are numerous ways to communicate with the Angels of Love and, by extension, with God. This chapter focuses on one of those methods of communication: *manifestation*.

Manifestation Basics

Manifestation is the opposite of releasement, a technique we discussed in the previous chapter. Manifestation is the art of bringing what you desire to fruition through Divine intervention. Here, you will learn the various tools of manifestation and use them to start attracting your life partner.

You will, in essence, be creating an order for God to fulfill. You want your order form to be as specific as possible to ensure that your match is perfect for you. This is where the lists you created in the first chapter will really help you. The closer your manifestation is to your heart's desire, the happier you will be with the outcome.

It may be hard for you to imagine that you need to place an order with God, a Being Who knows all. It's true that God knows the man or woman who would be perfect for you. However, if you had been instantly placed next to that person from birth, what lessons would you have learned? Is a life without lessons really one worth living?

Up to this point, you've learned many very important lessons—some of which you just spent time graduating from in the previous chapter. Now you've earned the right to settle down with a partner who will help you fulfill your true mission in life. You, in turn, will help your new partner fulfill his or her life purpose as well, so be prepared for a relationship in which you give as much as you receive. If you're the type of person who wants to only receive or wants to only give, we recommend spending additional time on the previous chapter before moving on.

The purpose of specificity is the old catch-22 of free will cropping up again. Take your parents, for example. Throughout your childhood, they probably had a much better idea of what you needed (versus what you wanted) than you did. You are, however, your own person. It would have been unfair for them to force their worldview on you once you'd grown up. Just as you needed space to mature and become a young adult, God has given you the freedom to become a remarkable human being. To avoid stomping on your free will, your Creator has given you a powerful gift that comes with a very strong warning—and this gift is manifestation.

Manifestation is a way for God to provide for you in all ways. The strong warning is that God will provide whatever you ask for, whether it's good for you or not. When you ask for things that are for your highest good, you generally receive a very reasonable facsimile of what you originally specified. When you ask for something negative, whether intentionally or not, God attempts to soften the blow.

Manifestation vs. Prayer

Manifestation differs from prayer in that you're not entering into a conversation with God to invite Divine intervention into your life. You're merely going along with what some people refer to as "the cosmic flow." When you practice manifestation, something is happening every minute of every day.

With manifestation, unlike prayer, you generally do get what you ask for, provided that it's something positive. But it may not be the best thing for you.

For instance, going back to the earlier example of the cheeky fellow who brought up the song "Mercedes Benz," we could change the song from a prayer to a manifestation. Instead of beseeching the Divine for this new car, we could use the manifestation tools you'll learn about later in this chapter. Then the chances of receiving this car instantly increase many times over.

However, what if that car ends up being a source of pain? Perhaps the car costs more to run and maintain than the owner can deal with. Or maybe it attracts too much attention, and the person feels uncomfortable to the point of no longer driving it. The outcome is that even though this individual received the car, he or she is not necessarily happy with it.

It's unlikely that there's an exact one-to-one correspondence between what people attract and the negative things they are focused on manifesting; however, they will generally have more negative slants to their lives. Watch those who are extremely negative, and see if their lives are ones you'd like to live. Typically, when you look at the lives of negative people, you find much hardship and lack, or anger and unhappiness.

For this reason, you must endeavor to be constantly vigilant in your manifestations. You can do so by always being aware of your thoughts, words, and actions. If you strive to be positive as much as possible, you will attract much more good energy.

You can see, then, how you must balance prayer and manifestation to bring about a happy result. Use them in concert to get close to your actual desire. We tell you this so that when you start learning and using the tools in this chapter, you'll understand that even though they're incredibly powerful, they do have limitations.

Just as you're unlikely to get everything you want through prayer if you don't truly need it, you're also unlikely to fully appreciate those things you acquire through manifestation alone. The question, then, remains: Why use manifestation at all if prayer can achieve similar results without the risks? The answer, as you might expect, is quite complicated.

Studies have shown that it really doesn't matter who the supplicants are or what their personal belief structures are. As long as people are sincere, prayer will be effective. However, it carries with it a certain stigma that some individuals are unable to get past.

For example, some people were brought up to believe that there's only one way to pray and have already rejected that mode. Also, while prayer is extraordinarily effective, many prefer a more hands-on approach to life. They'd rather risk getting something they may later regret by manifesting it if it means they get to choose what it is they'll receive.

Last, and most important, manifestation is something people do anyway. Every thought you think and every word you speak is essentially an act of manifestation. If you prefer to rely primarily on prayer, that's great. If not, we offer the following tips and techniques to ensure a bountiful manifestation.

Manifestation Techniques

As we stated earlier, the more specific you are in asking for what you want, the greater the likelihood that you'll receive it. There are several ways to refine your specific desires. You already used one of these important methods when you started your lists in Step 1. They helped you distill your desires to their core essences. Writing down your desires and continually refining them is a wonderful method of practicing specificity.

Go back to the lists you created. Is there anything you'd like to add to any of them? Anything you'd like to remove? Think of all the items you've listed and see how they interact with each other. Does the idea of a casual relationship with a wonderful person really sound so appealing now? Or would you rather push forward for the *lifelong* relationship?

Once you've refined your lists, keep them close, because all those details will come into play soon. These are the only mandatory tools in the upcoming exercises. All the others mentioned are optional and should be used only if you feel strongly guided to call on them.

Visualization

The first tool is visualization, which is employed to help keep you focused on those things you want to bring into your life. Here's a brief explanation of how it works. (This technique is discussed in greater detail in *Angels of Abundance*.)

Basically, visualization is the art of calling into being a picture of exactly what you want to manifest. (Some people find it easier to look at a representation of the person or object they desire before attempting this technique.) Try to recall the object or person in as much detail as possible. This visualization may seem trivial, but it does take a bit of practice to see things in your mind with a high degree of detail.

Visualization works by giving your mind a single focus to work with. It eliminates external distractions so that you're more likely to obtain the precise object of your desires. You are, in essence, visualizing all the time, but when you focus on one particular object, all the power is channeled into one space.

Building or obtaining a representation of a person based on a list of desired characteristics is a bit tricky. The best place to start is by drawing a picture. Depending on your artistic ability, the picture may not be a masterpiece, but it can still be effective.

See if you can create a picture that contains all the desired traits you wrote down. If a particular trait isn't physical, come up with some representation of that trait. For example, if you desire someone who is well-off financially, include a fancy car, money bags, or other identifiable symbols of wealth.

If you have absolutely no desire to draw a picture, find a photograph in a magazine that bears a resemblance to the person you're trying to attract. This should be an anonymous photograph, rather than a picture of a celebrity. When you look at this photo, think "man" or "woman," rather than "Kevin" or "Cindy."

Once you've developed a reasonable approximation of the type of person you want in your life, study the picture. Really get to know this person so that he or she is in your mind. If it's a simple drawing, use your imagination to fill in the holes. Try your very best to conjure a person out of this drawing. If you have a picture, allow the features to become a bit fainter, making them more ambiguous in your mind's eye so that you're not thinking of the particular individual in the photograph. This allows your mind to fill in any details of your soul mate's particular features as you begin to visualize them. It's okay if you find the man or woman in the photograph attractive. After all, it would be unusual to try to manifest a partner you weren't attracted to. But try to avoid being stuck on someone in particular.

The next step involves sitting down someplace quiet and comfortable. Play music if you like, and adjust the lighting to whatever level you're comfortable with. This place should have no outside interference. Try to stay undisturbed for at least five minutes.

Quiet your mind and slow your breathing. This time is all about you. Take several deep breaths and purge all extraneous thoughts from your mind.

Now call this picture into being in your mind. Envision this person in as much detail as possible, including aromas and textures. Once you're comfortable seeing this person as if he or she were really there, imagine walking up to the person and giving him or her a hug. Really see yourself and this person together, happy. The more realistic it feels, the more powerful the manifestation will be. Trust that this tool was created by God and given to you by the angels so that you never have to be without the man or woman you desire ever again.

Spend as much time with this person as you wish. Eventually you'll be together for eternity, so spending time like this can be great practice. If you're well practiced in visualization, it can even be a good testing ground to see if you really do enjoy the traits you've selected for this person.

If you feel tired or have simply had enough visualizing, feel free to stop at any time. Be gentle to yourself as you come back. Stretch out each muscle, don't stand up too quickly, and hydrate yourself adequately. Write down whatever thoughts, feelings, and emotions came to you while you were performing this technique. Do you have anything to add or subtract from your list? Did you imagine someone who was similar to your picture? If not, consider revising it as your visualizations lead you closer and closer to the specific person for you. It's perfectly fine to do so as needed. By making adjustments, you begin to hone your visualization, creating a stronger tool for drawing your desire to you like a magnet.

You can use this technique as often as you like. The more you do, the more powerful it becomes, and the more progress you'll make toward finding your soul mate. We don't recommend using this technique if you're feeling low, depressed, or negative. Those emotions can affect the visualization, which could have long-lasting implications. If you wish to practice this technique but aren't in the best place, try praying first. Pray for happiness, wholeness, and health. See if you can engage God in a conversation to elevate your mood. Once you're feeling better, take up this technique again if you so desire.

Visions of Love

This story was submitted by Janine from Wisconsin, who had an admittedly bad habit of dating only "jerks." She felt that normal guys were just too boring for her. However, she would always end up getting her heart broken by these guys or breaking up with them. Why? Because in her mind, they were jerks, of course!

Janine had finally had enough. She wanted to find someone responsible, respectful, and courteous. However, he couldn't be boring! Even though she'd realized the error of her ways, she still wanted some of that old excitement in her life. She wasn't quite sure how to go about this, though, since she thought that the two desires were mutually exclusive.

One day while browsing at a local bookstore, Janine came across a small handbook on the topic of visualization. She'd never heard of this technique before but was instantly drawn to it. After reading the handbook, she learned quite a bit about visualization in a very short period of time and began to follow this guidance.

Using one of the techniques in the book, she made a vision board. She placed on it pictures and drawings of people having a great time and looking happy. She also included pictures of romantic scenes and weddings. She would look at this vision board and substitute her own image for those of the women in the pictures. She was able to really see herself there and imagine what it would be like to experience that kind of happiness.

Shortly thereafter, Janine met someone under surprising circumstances. She was in line at an amusement park with her mother when she noticed a very attractive man in front of her. They started talking, laughing, and getting along well. When they reached the front of the line, the man running the ride asked, "How many?" The man casually responded, "Two," giving her a nice big smile. They ended up sitting together on the ride.

Two years later, Janine reports that they're still happy together and having lots of fun and spontaneous adventures. They go back to that amusement park on each anniversary to celebrate that fortuitous roller-coaster ride.

Janine was wise enough to follow her guidance on several occasions in this story. First, she was drawn to the handbook on visualization and acted upon her intuition. Next, she didn't just let it sit on her bookshelf, but studied the book and learned the lessons it contained. Then she used what she'd learned to create a simple and practical tool to help her focus her energies. Finally, she recognized her attraction to this man as a sign from the Angels of Love, and again, she acted. The end result was a happy, respectful, and fun relationship.

Positive Affirmations

Remember that you're not limited to using visualization. There are many techniques that work in a complementary fashion. For example, affirmations, the very powerful tool introduced in Step 1, may come in quite handy when trying to manifest your soul mate.

Affirmations tend to work best when you use them on a regular basis. You can post sticky notes with affirmations around your home so you'll remember to read or say them whenever you pass by. Some people like to recite their affirmations in the shower. Getting into the habit of revisiting them again and again makes them much more powerful.

The potential of humans and the human mind is infinite. What limits us is the ego. The ego is, generally speaking, the sum of all our fears. If your mind has ever told you that you're not good enough, not pretty enough, or not rich enough to fulfill your life purpose, then you're already familiar with the ego. None of these statements are true, of course, but they'll give you a wonderful excuse not to try.

For the purposes of this step, this would be a great starter affirmation:

I am worthy of happiness and emotional fulfillment. I enter willingly into this loving and enduring relationship. My perfect soul mate is coming to me now. This new relationship is fulfilling and mutually respectful.

You can shorten or lengthen this affirmation as you see fit. The only real rule is that the affirmation be framed in the most positive way possible. This is not the time or place for doubt or expressions of so-called realism. When you state these affirmations, you're recognizing the fact that linear time, as we know it, is only a human-made creation. These things you're saying are true in spiritual truth, even if you don't perceive them in that way at this particular juncture.

Discovery through Hypnosis

Another wonderful, if not quite so hands-on, method is hypnotic suggestion. This technique is similar to an affirmation in that it's designed to essentially convince you that a statement or situation is true. It's unlikely that you'll be able to perform this technique on yourself. However, there has been a tremendous resurgence of interest in professional hypnosis in recent times. Whatever stereotypical images hypnosis brings to mind, please discard them. Hypnosis is not the same as the chicanery of stage magicians. Rather, it's a powerful technique that can be used for a variety of therapeutic purposes.

Hypnosis may be helpful in this instance because it can allow you to get to the root of your desires. It can bypass your ego and help you realize what is truly in your heart, as opposed to the societal expectations that you have internalized.

Hypnotic suggestion can help you find your soul mate because it can be used to overcome shyness or personality traits that have blocked you from relationships in the past. It can also help show you the exact personality traits you most desire in another person. In this way, you're able to focus on what you want, rather than wasting time with those things you never really had an interest in anyway.

You can find reputable hypnotherapists by getting referrals from New Thought establishments, holistic health centers, or directories from certification boards for your area. As with all specialists, it pays to shop around and find one whom you resonate with before you proceed. If it's your first time visiting a hypnotherapist, bring someone you trust with you to alleviate any fears you may have.

Your Spiritual Toolbox

With the combined power of prayer, visualizations, affirmations, and hypnosis, you can accomplish just about anything. Not only are you taking the bull by the horns and using your own energy and positivity to help bring into being that which you desire, but you've called upon the Divine to assist you as well.

These tools do work, usually quite quickly, and in time you'll be able to use these techniques to attract not only your soul mate—something you will need to do only once—but anything else you desire as well.

DO YOUR LIFE-PARTNER LEGWORK

Finding Your Soul Mate

It's very unlikely that your new partner will just randomly ring your doorbell. It can happen, of course—and if you selected "UPS driver" as a desired trait in a mate, then your chances of that happening go up exponentially. However, for everyone else, a little legwork will be necessary to complete the task of finding your soul mate.

Looking for Love in All the Right Places

Where you find your partner will have a lasting impact on your future relationship. Not only are certain types of people drawn to certain types of places, but there's a chance that you'll spend more time in the location where you met. So try not to go to places where you feel uncomfortable or that you disapprove of. If you don't enjoy bars, for example, heading to one to pick up a partner would be a bad idea. Not only would you potentially find someone who has alcohol-dependency issues, but in all likelihood the person would continue going to bars once you're together. The same goes for dance clubs, sporting events, and religious gatherings. If you don't have a natural affinity for those sorts of places, then don't go out of your way to meet your partner there.

However, if you *do* have particular interests—no matter how unusual you consider them to be—you can have great luck meeting others who share them by going to gatherings designed around them. You can find events related to almost any activity by visiting sites such as Facebook and Meetup. You may be surprised by how many people in your local area have the same interests you do.

The importance of sharing activities and interests with your partner shouldn't be discounted. All too often people seek mates based on superficial attractions or because the other person is in some way exciting. While this is just fine if you're playing around, it's a terrible basis for a long-term relationship.

Sooner or later those habits you once found charming or exciting will become a source of irritation if your personality types are too different. Conversely, if you try to force yourself into a more subdued lifestyle by finding a very straitlaced, clean-cut person, at some point you'll find that you're bored to tears. Be honest with yourself regarding your values and interests, and you'll have a much happier, enduring relationship.

Venturing Out to Meet Your Soul Mate

Before you go out to find your new partner, there are a couple of things you can do to help improve your odds. Since you're dealing with another person who has an individual set of values, lifestyle choices, and emotions, the Angels of Love cannot force this person to be with you, regardless of how well matched you are. However, they have the power to assist you in making your own connection. You know by now that the Angels of Love cannot, nor would they if they could, interfere with your free will or that of another person.

(By the same token, neither should you interfere with anyone else's free will. At no time should you even entertain the idea of a love spell or potion. Not only do these generally not work but in some cases they can be extraordinarily dangerous. The tools and techniques mentioned here have been devised only to help change you for the better and to ensure that you're at the right place at the right time to meet your soul mate. These tools cannot force people into anything against their will.)

The first thing you should do before you venture out is pray. Even though you may be going to a social event, your goal is to get something accomplished. Asking for help from above will assist you with any task, especially one as critical to your life purpose as finding a soul mate. Here's an example of how you can ask for Heavenly help:

God, please send Your Angels of Love to me now. I desire Your loving intervention in helping me find my life partner. As I enter this place, please keep me safe from those whose intentions do not match my own. Please help me have the courage to interact with my future partner.

Please keep Your Angels of Love near me at all times so that I may receive loving guidance. Please tell me very clearly how best to proceed.

Thank You for Your continued presence.

Saying this prayer before you go to a new place will help keep you on the path to success throughout your new adventure. Unfortunately, the dating scene can involve people whose intentions and long-term goals don't align with yours. This prayer will go a long way toward protecting you from those individuals. Obviously your chances of finding people who are on the same page as you are increase if you avoid the typical places people go to find dates, such as bars and clubs.

Dating Criteria

When you first start looking for a new partner, it can be a very daunting prospect. This is especially true if you've been single for a significant period of time or if being single for a lengthy period makes you feel distressed. Dating, like any other skill, becomes easier the more you work at it. Soon you will no longer feel intimidated or overwhelmed when going out to find your life partner.

You must reframe your dating criteria to move this process along:

— **First**, you'll no longer be looking for a casual date, so you'll probably seek a different type of person than you did before. Physical appearance, while important, shouldn't be the *most* important thing here. What's most important is that the person fits as many criteria as possible on your list from Step 1.

— **Second**, the person should be stable, emotionally capable of being in a long-term relationship, and compatible with you. Opposites certainly do attract, but they rarely stay together for very long.

— A **third** crucial criterion that shouldn't be overlooked is that this partner *must* be single already. It doesn't matter if people claim that their partners don't understand them, or that they're going to leave the relationship. If they're not currently single (and generally speaking, separated doesn't count unless divorce proceedings have been initiated), stay far away from them. God and the Angels of Love aren't in the business of breaking up families, so you shouldn't play any part in that. We believe this scenario is so common that we felt the need to word this as strongly as we have.

Now we must insist on a pinkie swear from you that you won't get involved with an unavailable partner. Deal? Great. Moving on . . .

Courage to Connect

Courage and confidence have a lot to do with how you find your mate. You're potentially dealing with someone who's just as intimidated by you as you are by him or her. When seeking a lifelong partner, traditional roles such as those dictating who may approach whom do not mean as much as they did when you were just looking for a casual partner.

This is especially true when it comes to spiritual events. Men who attend are generally very conscious of the fact that they're in the minority and tend to behave in an introverted way. If you're a woman, even though these men might love to approach you and strike up a conversation, they'd never do anything to violate a woman's boundaries. If a woman is interested in a man at one of these events, it's imperative that she give him a subtle but clear gesture indicating that she wants to talk to him.

We've attended and staffed a multitude of spiritual events around the world where we've met hundreds of men. By and large, they're the greatest bunch of guys imaginable, but many are also beset by conflicted feelings that don't improve their odds of finding a life partner. Even though they're 100 percent compatible with so many of the women in attendance, these men are petrified of rejection or of offending a member of the opposite sex. This fear, combined with women's societal expectations that men should approach them, creates a perfect-storm situation where people who are very eager for a connection end up just staring at each other without speaking. This situation also applies to same-sex partners.

Obviously something needs to change at these spiritual events and other meetups where reticence prevails, and we hope that *you* will be the one to instigate that change! Somebody, at some point, needs to say *something*, and it may as well be you. Put aside any worries that you may be intruding or that your advances are unwelcome. That will be immaterial at that moment. All you have to do is start a conversation with this person. You may find that you have quite a bit in common if you take the time to get to know each other.

The same is true for almost any mind-body-spirit gathering. Singles go to these events to meet people precisely because the attendees are so different from the mainstream dating crowd. Therefore, don't make the mistake of expecting to find someone who has more conventional tendencies at one of these gatherings. If, for example, you want to meet a guy who will approach you and do all the talking, you can find him easily at any bar in the world. If, on the contrary, you're looking for a devoted partner who will actually listen to you and care what you have to say, then you may have to accept the fact that he will not aggressively approach you.

Patience and Perseverance

One thing to keep in mind is that you've done a remarkable job laying the groundwork for finding a soul mate so far. Keep up the good work, even when you're out meeting new people. Don't settle for the first person you make contact with, unless he or she *is* the person you've been manifesting.

Melissa: Some people get to the point where they believe that it's better to be with the wrong partner than with nobody at all. Prior to Grant and I meeting each other, we both fell into this way of thinking in our past relationships. The Angels of Love helped us think differently! Therefore, while we can certainly empathize with this logic, that doesn't make it true. When you're in a relationship with the wrong person—whether casual or committed—you run the risk that the right person will pass you by, considering you unavailable and falsely believing that you're as happy as you pretend to be. Remember that God and the Angels of Love are helping you find the right mate, but the responsibility of being patient until that individual comes along belongs to you alone.

When You Think You've Met Your Soul Mate

You will generally know whom you're supposed to approach once you arrive at your chosen location. You may just sense something about that person or simply have a magnetic pull drawing you to him or her. If you're feeling guided to talk to that man or woman, then you must initiate a conversation.

The Angels of Love are helping you along by giving you small nudges, such as an unusually strong attraction or the desire to find out what that person is all about. By paying attention to these signs, you can see in which direction you're being guided.

At the same time, it's critically important to pay attention to any and all red flags you may notice. These are warning signs from above, so heed them! The most important thing is that you keep your own counsel throughout this process. Your friends and loved ones may mean well, but only *you* will be receiving the Divine guidance you've asked for. In other words, you will be the only reliable judge of whether or not you and this person are meant for each other.

If you are doubting your ability to understand your guidance, once again you can ask the Angels of Love to bring you clarity during your dream time. Remember, when you awaken in the morning, write down the messages you received in your journal. As you begin to understand what your guidance is telling you, you will know the direction and steps you need to take with the people you are meeting.

Sooner or later you'll get into a conversation with someone you feel is your soul mate. That's a great first step, but now is the time to really shine. You don't want to deceive this person in any way, but you must also be aware that he or she is evaluating you, too. This is not the moment to say that you've been trying to manifest a soul mate. If it comes up, you should discuss your spirituality as you would *any* important part of your life. Be very careful, however, if you choose to share that you're looking for your life partner. This can scare some people off, especially if you've just met. On the other hand, it can be a great tactic to get those you're *not* interested in to back off.

The relatively brief time you have with this person should be spent wisely. By all means, dance and have a good time if that's what the venue offers, but find some shared ground that you can connect with him or her on. And definitely get the person's contact information!

Too many times we've witnessed great love connections at spiritual events, but when we check on the two parties a month later, we're told that the individuals never bothered to get each other's e-mail addresses or phone numbers. They assumed that if it were meant to be, they'd be magically placed together again someday. While that's a charmingly romantic notion, it's one that is guaranteed to cause more emotional angst than the average person is prepared to endure. Besides, the Angels of Love opened a door of opportunity for you, and it is up to you to take the action to step through it. So make finding a way to contact this person again one of your top goals.

If you and this person really feel you are each other's soul mate—fantastic! However, it's time to be patient once again. If this person truly is your intended, then the feelings will last beyond that day. You're not meant to keep this person waiting as some sort of bizarre test, but it's a great idea to get some distance from the situation to see if this really could be Mr. or Ms. Right—and not just Mr. or Ms. Right Now. Particularly if alcohol is involved, waiting—even a little while—is a must before jumping into any sort of relationship. Take time to get to know each other first by communicating over the phone, through e-mail exchanges, or by spending some time among groups of people.

When All Else Fails . . .
"Let Go and Let God"

If you're unable to find your soul mate, don't despair. It simply means you're going to have to try again. If that sounds exhausting to you, then take a bit of a break. You're much more likely to find your life partner when you're in a positive, energetic mood than when you're in an exhausted, depressed one. Frankly, most people find talking with a depressed person quite a turnoff. But you shouldn't feel guilty about being depressed. That's something that most people go through sooner or later. However, you should seek help for any lasting depression through religious, spiritual, or therapeutic counseling. As covered in Step 2, you must make yourself ready to be in a relationship first.

Some people have shared with us that they've tried so many times to find someone that they've completely given up. "Great!" we say to that. It's far better to leave this part of your life in the hands of the Divine and go about your daily business than to get into a negative space about it. We're blessed to be favored children of an infinitely powerful and loving God.

This means that sometimes when you leave those difficult parts of your life in Divine hands, they can work out much better than if you were to worry over them yourself. As is often said, you can find the best things in life when you're not looking.

Divine Communication

Regardless of whether you choose a hands-on approach to finding your new life partner or not, a continual dialogue with God is the best way to have a balanced life in all respects. When you communicate regularly with your Divine Creator, you're much more likely to follow the guidance that we're all given every day. This will ultimately lead you to your perfect partner.

Like-Minded

This story comes from Natalie in Southern California, whose unsatisfying dating history is representative of an all-too-common phenomenon in urban environments. Natalie is a very sensitive and gentle person whose greatest passion in life is caring for horses and dolphins. She says that she can't handle harsh energies.

This is understandable, but she wrote to us that nearly every guy she met in Southern California was too harsh for her. She described them as thugs who had no interest in a long-term, equal partnership. She was so stricken by the negative energies she received from the typical guys in her area that she started to prefer the company of animals to people in general.

Natalie's family continually pressured her to date, even trying to set her up on numerous occasions. It wasn't that she relished being single, but she didn't want to be with someone she was afraid of or who she knew was lying to her. Sometimes she'd just wait for the dates to be over so she could go back to doing what she actually enjoyed.

Natalie was so desperate to end these horrendous experiences that she started praying. She begged and pleaded for God to either send her the right person or send nobody at all. She felt it would be easier to be alone forever than to put up with pushy men whom she couldn't relate to.

Natalie says she was brought up to believe that prayers have the most power when spoken in church. So she decided to go to her local place of worship, and once she did, she realized something she'd forgotten long ago: there were other people who thought like she did, even in the middle of her large city.

It wasn't long before Natalie met a wonderful man she didn't have to be afraid of. She said that he was a gentle soul, just like her, but that she also felt very protected by him. Today, she still enjoys horses and dolphins and is now able to share these interests with someone she cares deeply for.

It was very fortunate for Natalie that she started going to church again. Not only did she meet a wonderful man but she was able to reconnect with a spiritual community of like-minded individuals. Often in big cities, it can get very lonely even if someone is constantly surrounded by others.

Dating Rules Recap

Summing up this chapter in easy-to-manage bites:

- Try to meet people only at places you actually want to go to or feel drawn to.

- Pray for protection and guidance.

- Be the one to break the ice. Don't let shyness or social barriers block you from your future partner.

- Pay attention to those signs that are guiding you to the right people.

- Pay even more attention to those signs warning

you off the wrong individuals. Don't settle for the wrong person just to be in a partnership.

- Try, try again. If you feel put off, uneasy, or exhausted, ask God and the Angels of Love for help.

If you follow these very simple steps, we can just about guarantee that you'll find your perfect partner. Of course, the timing of it all is up to you and your Creator. Feel free to renegotiate the necessary time line at any point. Anything that inspires you to communicate with God is a great thing, even if it's just to whine and complain a bit, which is fine in prayer as you are conversing with your Creator. That is the sort of loving devotion you should also seek in your romantic relationship.

STEP 5

BE PRESENT IN YOUR PARTNERSHIP

Keeping Your Relationship Intact

Now that you've gotten through the difficult part of finding a relationship in the first place, you have the very important task of keeping this relationship intact forever. It's not as much work as it seems. Or, more to the point, it's not *supposed* to be as much work as it seems. In fact, it essentially boils down to just three things: *communication*, *shared experiences*, and *tending the garden of romance*.

Even if you haven't manifested your perfect partner by this step (which, most likely, you have not in one reading of this book), this is still an important chapter for you to read. As you think about the tools in this chapter and put your focus on a healthy and enduring partnership, you will be more prepared and aligned with your intention for a soul-mate relationship.

Keeping a relationship solid is not something that anyone can do by him- or herself. It would be foolish to even try. It takes *two* people working together every single day. It's not a specific action, but the sum of *all* actions, that shows how hard you're both endeavoring to keep your relationship viable.

Most of us have been in a past relationship that just seemed to fall apart. Perhaps on paper the relationship looked fine, but there was no substance to it. The only thing holding the two of you together was the very fact that you *were* together. It was just easier to be in the relationship than to put the energy into getting out. That is the essence of a failed relationship: it has so little energy that it can't even motivate you to leave it.

So what happened in that relationship? The bottom line is: someone stopped trying. It could have been you, the other person, or even both of you. It doesn't matter, because that relationship served a very important function: it taught you what *not* to do. Now, having gone through a relationship where both partners weren't working at it, you know to avoid that sort of situation in the future.

Of course, you can't force someone to be present in a relationship. You can, however, take some decisive steps to reduce the chances of getting to the point where someone has checked out of the relationship in the first place.

Open Communication

The most important priority from the very beginning is *communication*—nothing is more beneficial for the longevity of a relationship. The less a couple talks, the more likely it is that the relationship will be filled with frustration, annoyances, anger, hurt, and jealousy.

Cultivating Closeness

Melissa: People have asked what Grant and I do to have such a loving relationship, so here we will share a few things.

We like to begin and end our day with each other, which we have done from the start of our relationship. Many people are astonished when we tell them we always wake up together. We explain how the other stays in bed until the sleeping one awakens. If one of us needs to set an alarm to get up early, the other gets up too. People may laugh, but morning time is important to us; it's how we begin our day—and we want to begin our day together. We awaken with a smile, then discuss our dreams. After that, no matter how short or long a time we have for breakfast, we eat together. We share our goals for the day, laugh over news, or discuss decisions that need to be made. It's our time together, and it's precious.

Grant and I take time to play at the end of each workday (sometimes during a break, like lunch), even if it's just for five minutes. That's right! We play and laugh. Silliness and playfulness is a key component to partnership. Enjoyment and merrymaking help balance any seriousness in the world. Playing also offers you and your partner time to express all sides of yourself.

Around dinnertime we talk about our day, sharing stories, thoughts, ideas, things we have accomplished, and what we would like to accomplish. We eat dinner together every night.

Some partners may not be able to always do this, but at least making it a priority is a relationship enhancer. Again, it's our time together to laugh, talk, and share.

Grant and I have never spent one night apart. When bedtime calls to us, we go together. We feel it's important to complete our day together in our sacred chamber (bedroom). It's where we began our day, so we like to go full circle, waking up and falling asleep in each other's company. We keep bed topics about love, sharing, and laughing. No serious stuff here, as this is our intimate, romantic space. We do not keep devices in our bedroom such as a television, phones, or other electronics, except a soothing alarm when needed. We find such items distracting to relationships, causing interruptions in intimacy.

We all want our partners to treat us with a certain degree of respect, but unless we communicate what that means to us, they may never know how to meet our needs. So often people really must to be *told* what we want so that they'll give it to us.

Likewise, if you notice that your partner isn't able to speak to you about his or her desires, try to initiate a conversation to reopen the channels of communication. The more you improve your level of communication, the happier you will both be.

True communication can be possible only when both partners are on an even footing. If one partner is continually getting angry with the other, fear can develop. Fear is an impediment not only to communication but also to love. It's impossible to love that which you fear; the emotions are completely at odds with each other. This can't be stressed enough. Open communication must be expressed without anger, fear, or intimidation.

A great tool to help both you and your partner talk and listen to each other is physical touch. For example, touching your partner's shoulder, hand, back, or arm when discussing an issue, bringing up something exciting, or expressing your feelings is a great way to connect on a deeper level. Your partner is more likely to really listen to you. In turn, you are more likely to feel you had his or her attention. Physical touch brings partners a greater sense of connection and healing.

Men and women generally have very different communication styles. These differences must be accommodated in male-female relationships. Men typically want to solve problems that come up in conversation and then be done with the matter. Women, on the other hand, are more likely to ask detailed questions and want to talk about the issue for extended periods of time. You can see how these two styles can conflict with each other. For men, it's critical to learn how to listen without offering solutions or tuning out. For women, it's equally important to remember that this isn't a girlfriend they're talking to. There will be a certain point when they will have to let the matter drop without overanalyzing.

Conflict Resolution

A helpful tool to keep your conversation to the point and find resolution quickly is to set a timer. That's right, ladies—or men—who like to talk about an issue until dawn! A phone stopwatch, egg timer, or any timer will work.

1. The person who wants to discuss a topic begins. Set the timer to five minutes. This allows you to make your point succinctly. When the timer is up, your turn is over.

2. Set the timer again, this time allowing your partner to repeat back what they heard you say in the way in which they heard it. Allow them to say it in their own words, not regurgitating yours. With the time

remaining on the timer, your partner tells you how they feel about what you have said.

3. Then, set the timer again for five minutes, this time allowing you to comment.

You can go back and forth like this for up to 30 minutes. By that point, you should have something resolved. Thank your partner for taking time to discuss the issue.

Relationship Repair

Revitalizing communication can help jump-start a stalled relationship as well. Starting the process can be very difficult, but the end results make it worthwhile. Marriage counseling has its merits, but there's nothing more powerful for a relationship than two people sitting down and discussing their life together. They may find that old anger, regrets, or other negativity has been hanging between them for some time. While it might seem as if bringing these things into the open makes them worse, this isn't true. They were there all along, and all the partners have done is shine a spotlight on them so they can be tended to.

There's no such thing as an irreparable relationship unless one party refuses to take responsibility for his or her share. In nearly every situation—barring a sudden onset of mental illness or cases of addiction—both parties are responsible in some way for the breakdown. Anyone who assumes that he or she has done everything right and the other partner has done everything wrong isn't being honest. Taking a genuine look at the state of the relationship will give you insights that can help you realize where it went wrong, and thus where it can be fixed. This is accomplished only through communication.

Communication will also keep a healthy, loving relationship on the right track. If you take a proactive approach toward your love life and keep the lines of communication open, you can be assured that your relationship will remain healthy and loving. That is not to say that you may not encounter small issues from time to time, but they'll be rectified easily and without undue hardship. The more you and your partner communicate, the better you'll get to know each other. A great goal to shoot for is a lifelong relationship where you learn something new about your partner every single day. That keeps life a great adventure and makes living with your partner an absolute joy.

Achieving Balance

In a loving, healthy relationship, nobody's in charge. At no point should one partner nag or browbeat or try to dominate the other. That's a sign of an unbalanced relationship that's sorely in need of proper communication. Rather, each partner should be happy to contribute equally to the union.

However, *equal* can mean different things to different people. For example, some people have an aversion to doing the dishes. Trust us, if your partner's mother couldn't make him or her do them, *you* have little chance of succeeding. Perhaps for a while your partner will be happy to do the dishes because it makes you happy, but sooner or later that old aversion will rear its head. This isn't the time to get angry; it's the time to find a way for your partner to contribute that makes him or her happy.

Certainly everyone would love to get out of doing certain chores, and if one partner doesn't like performing a particular task, the other person should do it. If taking on that extra work makes things unbalanced, shuffle chores around until each of you is doing something you enjoy, or at least something you don't loathe.

Similarly, simply being the breadwinner in the relationship doesn't excuse someone from contributing to the upkeep of the household. Neither does the fact that someone looks after the children more.

Another sign of an unbalanced relationship is when partners begin to badger one another, air their "dirty laundry," and make negative comments about each other in public. All issues should be kept private between the partners. Picking on each other in public, including in front of friends and family, is a sign of disrespect and disharmony in the relationship. In this case, you will need to sit down to discuss what tension is underlying your relationship.

Honesty in your relationship is another factor critical to staying together. Partners who keep secrets from each other will have added difficulties. In every area of your life, you should strive to be as open and honest with your partner as you can. You don't have to go into every little detail of your life before you became partners unless you want to. However, starting from the point when you came together, you should make an effort not to hide anything. When you stay honest, you have nothing to fear from your partner. You'll find that you'll both trust each other more and feel that you can open up completely, without deception or lies. Trust creates a beautiful bond between two people.

Defusing Disagreements over Money

It has been our experience that when finances are an issue, couples tend to argue more. The added stress of money worries can exacerbate an already tenuous situation. Often one partner will start an argument that neither person really cares about. He or she has just been pushed to the breaking point by external stress and is lashing out in frustration. This is an unfortunate situation that *can* be remedied.

The first step in preventing pointless fights is to take a breath, think, and figure out what's really upsetting you. Even the old standby of counting to 10 can help you figure out what, if anything, is actually wrong. The second step is to take a proactive stance in your finances, just as you have in your love life. You don't have to be a passive participant in the world of money any more than you do in the world of love. (The book *Angels of Abundance* shows how you can use tools and techniques very similar to those you've already learned here to improve your financial life.)

Shared Experiences

Another important matter to take into consideration is that God and the angels have put you two together and have the power to help you *stay* together. This isn't the time to forget about these Divine influences. Mutually shared spiritual experiences will go a long way toward helping you two grow in your relationship. This is not to say that you both must believe in precisely the same things. It's perfectly acceptable to have different worldviews, as long as each of you feels heard and respected.

Even if two partners have completely different spiritual beliefs, there are still numerous activities they can engage in for mutually satisfying spiritual gratification. For example, nearly every religion upholds a certain reverence for the beauty of nature. Hiking, watching a sunset, or even spending the day at the beach can be a spiritual experience for both partners. We encourage couples to experiment and find other ways in which they can share the wonders of creation with each other.

If you and your partner are quite similar in your spiritual views, there are many additional activities you can participate in together. A spiritually connected household is so much stronger than just two people living together. Even though you two may be having a blast, try to remember that you need spiritual fulfillment just as much as you need physical, emotional, and intellectual stimulation.

Tending the Garden of Romance

Saving the best for last, a *romantic* relationship is one that is most likely to endure for a lifetime. The most important thing to remember about romance is that it's a verb as well as a noun. You and your partner will both need to consciously take steps to keep your life together romantic. Set aside weekly date nights, go away for a weekend together, venture out to a nice restaurant, or take dance lessons together. When you have a complex relationship involving children, it can be very difficult to keep the romance alive. Typically this is only because some people don't value romance as much as they should. Yet if you tend to the garden of romance, you will not only be fulfilled in your relationship but you will teach your children how to cultivate a healthy, loving relationship themselves.

Regardless of how busy a person becomes, there are certain areas of life that simply must be attended to. Even a person with 10 children has to take certain steps to ensure his or her own sanity and survival. Well, what if we told you that the sanity and survival of your relationship is just as dependent upon your taking the steps to keep romance alive?

Doing one thing every single day—no matter how small—that shows your partner you still love, desire, and respect him or her will reap amazing results. Valentine's Day is great, but it is the foolish couple who tells each other how they feel only once a year. You may believe that you can't set aside the time to do this every day. We say you can't afford *not* to do this every day. After all, how much time does it take to repair a broken relationship—or, worse, find a new one? Give yourself permission to love your partner as regularly as you brush your teeth or change your clothes, without feeling guilty for taking this time.

No part of your life—including work, children, relatives, and education—is, or will be, more important than sharing tender, loving moments with each other. The fact is that you two are together, first and foremost, because you love each other.

Everyone in your life will benefit from seeing the loving, devoted example you set. Make this relationship the centerpiece of your existence.

Life—especially that which is lived with a committed partner—is a balancing act, one that, with a little bit of practice, you'll be able to manage without any difficulty. Just remember to call upon God and the angels whenever you feel you need some help.

We will begin tending to the garden of romance with this prayer:

> *God, thank You for helping my soul mate and me find each other. Please assist us in promoting a strong, healthy, loving relationship rooted in unconditional love that blossoms each day.*
>
> *Angels of Love, please continue to guide us in preserving and developing our perfect relationship. Help us to always keep our hearts and minds open to each other. Help us learn from, support, and nurture each other.*
>
> *We are open to all the Divine support and intervention necessary to allow us to maintain our ideal relationship.*

Thank You, God, the Divine master of love itself. Thank you, angels. We give gratitude and joyfully celebrate our loving relationship always.

AFTERWORD

Your Three Keys: Being Proactive, Prayerful, and Positive

God and the Angels of Love have provided several tools and techniques for you to use to find your soul mate. These tools are available to anyone at any time, regardless of background or personal beliefs. The fact that you're abundantly provided for in all ways should be a source of great comfort and joy.

The point of these exercises and tools—beyond their obvious use in manifesting your soul mate—is to prevent you from being merely a spectator in your own life. At all times, you must remember to take a proactive approach toward attaining those things you want. It's only when you give up and become a nonparticipant that you allow yourself to become a victim.

Surrendering and letting go is a very valuable tool. This doesn't mean, however, that you're not supposed to help yourself. It simply means letting go of a specific outcome, and then letting God and the angels make the best decisions for you. You're still allowed to talk, ask, pray, and affirm. There may even be times when you completely disagree with what has seemingly been chosen for you. In those cases, you must forge ahead and speak to your Creator.

All the spiritual tools you've learned about in this book or any other work are nothing more than different ways of speaking to God. Just as the angels are His messengers, so too are your thoughts, words, and actions. And visualization, affirmation, prayer, and positive thinking help ensure that you're sending out only the messages you wish to broadcast.

Similarly, the various stories in the previous chapters share a common thread—all those who were generous enough to submit their accounts followed the guidance they were given. None of them were gurus, monks, or nuns. They had no formal spiritual training but were able to pick up little tips here and there and use them to great personal benefit.

So remember that if you follow the guidance you receive from God and the angels, there are no closed doors. If you watch for signs and, most important, follow them, they will lead you to some wonderful places. All these people were on the verge of giving up when they decided to be open to Divine inspiration and create a happy ending for their stories. These people were kind enough to share their stories with us so that we can all learn something—or, at the very least, become inspired. It's a very personal thing—the sharing of one's story. We applaud the courage and generosity of these contributors.

We want to leave you with one last reminder: *stay positive.* Positivity is a very powerful force for change. Also, positive people naturally attract others, whereas negative people generally do not. Think back to a time when you tried to comfort and cheer up a friend who absolutely refused to be happy. That is a normal energetic reaction. The rest of the universe reacts similarly in the face of negativity. Sometimes things don't go as planned, so it's okay to express your frustration, doubt, anxiety, and other negative emotions. But don't let these negative feelings take over your life and your outlook.

Anytime you feel overwhelmed or fatalistic about what you're doing, it's time to take a break. So use the meditations in Step 2 and the Appendix, and make sure you pray and also relax.

Never let yourself lose sight of the real goal: finding happiness. If something isn't making you happy, stop doing it.

This work, like all of life, is an adventure. More specifically, it is *your* adventure. The more energy and enthusiasm you put into it, the more you will get out of it. Especially when speaking of love and romance, attitude is everything. The choice to have a positive and optimistic attitude is completely up to you, and choosing this path will definitely make you a happier and more loving person.

Finally, we want to thank you for daring to take this step to improve your life. Whether you're looking for a new relationship or you're interested in revitalizing your current one, doing what is necessary to make things better is a brave move. If you've learned something new—congratulations! We encourage you to try out what you've learned as soon as you can. The more you practice, the more successful you'll be. If, on the other hand, this is all old hat, then welcome back to the path, and remember that you cannot be reminded of your power too often or speak to God and the Angels of Love too much.

Thank you for reading!

APPENDIX

Meditations

You can come back to these meditations any time you are feeling blocked, overwhelmed, or even in need of some mental peace. Please refer to this section as often as you would like, as meditation can help with every step of this book. The process of finding a new life partner can be daunting. And with the help of God and the Angels of Love, there may be times when you just need to take a break. Even if the whole process is easy for you, there are still numerous benefits to taking a time-out.

Meditation is a remarkably effective and easy method of relaxing. It can not only help you take your mind off whatever may be troubling you, but it can give you the energy necessary to handle problems in a much more positive way.

Meditation is a great start and end to the day; it can give you the peace and energy to keep going in a spiritually charged way. It can also help you relax and prepare for a good night's sleep with meaningful dreams.

Like prayer, meditation is a way to connect with the Divine Source. It can quiet your mind so that you're able to hear God and the angels speaking to you. If you're ever in doubt about your current path or what to do next, meditation can and will help you gain some clarity.

Your conscious mind or ego doesn't deliberately set out to interfere with your life purpose and your ability to communicate. It has evolved in the way it has due to past hurts, insults, and doubts. It's attempting to protect you from further harm by preventing you from doing anything daring or out of the ordinary. This, however, is not truly living. Meditation allows you to bypass this part of your mind so that you can go forth courageously.

Please be gentle with yourself immediately before and after you meditate. Ease into and out of meditation slowly. You'll want to find a quiet, private place where you can meditate so that you get the most out of it. And try to avoid negative people afterward, as you'll be very open to their low-vibrational input.

Give yourself permission to really use meditation to your advantage, and enjoy the process.

Following are two sample meditations you can try as often as you'd like. One is a meditation to use when you first get out of bed to start your day in a strong, positive, and enthusiastic manner. The other will help you wind down from a busy day so that you can rest, relax, sleep, and dream peacefully.

Morning Meditation: Temple of Love

Find a place to sit or lie down. Close your eyes, open your palms to the sky, and relax. Take a nice deep breath, filling your entire body with air. Exhale, releasing all the air from your body. Again, inhale and exhale. Become aware of the rhythm of your breath inhaling and exhaling. Call upon the Angels of Love. Feel them around you as you breathe in their love.

In your mind's eye, you begin to see a beautiful white marble stairway before you. You notice that this majestic stairway has eight steps leading up to a beautiful temple. The number eight represents infinity. It is the symbol of the joining together of a soul-mate relationship and uniting love for eternity. As you begin to climb the stairway, you feel energized and excited about visiting this temple, and you feel guided to enter. As you take your last step up the stairway, a glorious white temple with four walls and a rounded-dome top comes into view before you. This shape represents the masculine and feminine.

You step through the doorway of the Temple of Love. You can sense that this is the beginning of a wonderful journey. You can feel your growing excitement, the beating of your heart, and the knowingness that all is orchestrated for your highest good. As you look around the temple, you notice that each wall is painted a different color. One wall is gold, representing the Divine connection within you. Another wall is pink, symbolizing unconditional love. The third wall is green, symbolizing the healing power of love. The fourth wall is silver, representing the heavens and the earth within you.

In the center of the temple, you see a large ruby. Around the stone are the Angels of Love. They welcome you to the center of the temple. Walking toward the Angels of Love, you can feel their powerful, soothing, loving energy. As you reach these angels, they surround and embrace you. You can feel unconditional love rushing through you. The angels motion for you to reach down and touch the ruby. You extend your hand and gently place it on the stone. You can feel deep-rooted love, passion, and your life-force energy coursing through you. The angels each give you a special message of love now. Listen carefully.

You thank them for the messages. One of the angels steps forward and looks into your eyes. You hear another message in your mind saying that you must first love yourself. You can feel that these Angels of Love are guiding you to your perfect soul mate—the relationship that is for your highest good and fulfills your heart's desires. You know with complete faith that God and the Angels of Love are helping you bring in the relationship you have longed for.

If you already share a loving relationship with your soul mate, God and the Angels of Love are guiding and supporting you both. They're helping your relationship continue on its path of beauty, unconditional love, joy, and discovery.

Taking your hand away from the ruby, you now sense the angels' light growing brighter. It surrounds you like a warm blanket and feels inspiring and supportive. Take a moment to breathe in this beautiful light. Your heart feels as if it's expanding to receive the love you deserve right now. As the angels' light grows brighter and brighter, you now find yourself back in this time, this place, this body . . .

Evening Meditation: The Gift

Sit or lie down in a comfortable place. Relax, open your palms to the sky, and close your eyes. Take a nice, deep inhalation, and then exhale completely. Take another deep inhalation, filling your lungs and your back with air. Completely release and exhale all the air from your body.

This time, as you inhale, see a beautiful green light coming from the center of the earth. Entering the soles of your feet, it moves up through your ankles, calves, and knees . . . up through your thighs, into your pelvis, up through your abdomen, and into your heart. As you exhale, a beautiful silver light comes down from the heavens, entering the top of your head. It moves down through your throat, shoulders, chest, and into your heart. Continue to inhale the green light, and exhale the silver light.

In your mind's eye, you begin to see a luminous circle of light in front of you. This light consists of the palest colors of blue, pink, green, yellow, and purple. You feel drawn to this light. You begin walking toward this beautiful circle of colors. As you approach, you feel the light surround and embrace you.

You feel safe, comforted, and supported. You notice that the light surrounding you begins to take shape. You see faces forming in this light—they are the Angels of Love. Take a moment to look in the angels' eyes. You can feel warmth, protection, support, and love radiating from each of them.

An angel steps forward and hands you a bright golden box. The box is empty. The Angels of Love are asking you to place all your relationship worries, cares, fears, and frustrations in this box. Take a moment to think about all the things you want to place in it. As you begin placing these things into the box, you feel relief flood over you. The weight of searching for a romantic relationship lifts off your shoulders. As you place the last care and worry into the box, you close the lid. You feel relieved and worry-free as you hand the angels the golden box. You know that these Angels of Love will now take this box with all your romance and relationship worries and concerns. They are relieving you of all your doubt and fears.

One by one, the Angels of Love embrace you. You feel calm and peacefulness emanating from the angel glowing with blue light. You feel soothed and comforted by the angel shining with yellow light. You feel unconditional love coming from the angel radiating pink light. You feel healing energy from the angel sparkling with green light. You feel deeply satisfied, knowing that all is well, as you gaze upon the angel aflame with purple light.

As the Angels of Love continue to embrace you, you know that everything will work out for the best. You can feel the deep and unconditional love, support, and help you're receiving. You have faith that all is being Divinely orchestrated with respect to your soul mate, your perfect relationship, and that which your heart truly desires. Your heart is soothed. Your mind is calm. Your body is relaxed. Your spirit is open to receiving. You know you can trust that the Angels of Love are helping you release your worries about your love relationship. You can trust that the Angels of Love are helping you find the partner who is perfect for you in all ways. As you fall asleep tonight, know that you're being held in the arms of the Angels of Love while you rest, relax, and rejuvenate . . .

ABOUT THE AUTHORS

Grant Virtue is attending school to obtain his doctorate of psychology, while also acting as the technical coordinator for Angel University LLC. Grant has studied spirituality, health, and law throughout his life. In addition to being the co-author of *Angel Words* and *Angels of Abundance* (with his mother, Doreen Virtue) and the author of *Living a Blessed Life,* he is currently working on a series of novels. Grant lives with his wife, Melissa, and their cat in Florida.

You can find him at www.GrantVirtue.com
or on Twitter: @GrantVirtue.

Melissa Virtue began studying dreams over 20 years ago. She leads workshops on dream interpretation and angels; created and teaches SpiralDance™, a spiritually based dance technique; and is the author of several works, including *Angel Dreams* and *Angel Dreams Oracle Cards* (with Doreen Virtue), *Dreamtime*, and the children's book series *Magical Dream Journeys.*

For more information about Melissa, please visit:
www.SacredSolas.com.

NOTES

Hay House Titles of Related Interest

YOU CAN HEAL YOUR LIFE, the movie, starring Louise Hay & Friends
(available as a 1-DVD program and an expanded 2-DVD set)
Watch the trailer at: www.LouiseHayMovie.com

THE SHIFT, the movie, starring Dr. Wayne W. Dyer
(available as a 1-DVD program and an expanded 2-DVD set)
Watch the trailer at: www.DyerMovie.com

~

*HOW TO LOVE YOURSELF (AND SOMETIMES OTHER PEOPLE):
Spiritual Advice for Modern Relationships,* by Lodro Rinzler
and Meggan Watterson (book)

LOVEABILITY: Knowing How to Love and Be Loved,
by Robert Holden, Ph.D. (book)

MEDIDATING: Meditations for Fearless Romance,
by Gabrielle Bernstein (audio)

NAKED!: How to Find the Perfect Partner by Revealing Your True Self,
by David Wygant (book)

*QUANTUM LOVE: Use Your Body's Atomic Energy to Create the
Relationship You Desire,* by Laura Berman, Ph.D. (book)

REWIRE YOUR BRAIN FOR LOVE: Creating Vibrant Relationships Using the Science of Mindfulness, by Marsha Lucas, Ph.D. (book)

SECOND FIRSTS: Live, Laugh, and Love Again, by Christina Rasmussen (book)

SECRETS OF ATTRACTION: The Universal Laws of Love, Sex, and Romance, by Sandra Anne Taylor (book)

SPIRIT-CENTERED RELATIONSHIPS: Experiencing Greater Love and Harmony Through the Power of Presencing, by Gay Hendricks, Ph.D., and Kathlyn Hendricks, Ph.D. (book-with-audio)

All of the above are available at your local bookstore, or may be ordered by contacting Hay House (see next page).

~

We hope you enjoyed this Hay House book. If you'd like to receive our online catalog featuring additional information on Hay House books and products, or if you'd like to find out more about the Hay Foundation, please contact:

Hay House, Inc., P.O. Box 5100, Carlsbad, CA 92018-5100
(760) 431-7695 or (800) 654-5126
(760) 431-6948 (fax) or (800) 650-5115 (fax)
www.hayhouse.com® • www.hayfoundation.org

Published and distributed in Australia by: Hay House Australia Pty. Ltd., 18/36 Ralph St., Alexandria NSW 2015 • *Phone:* 612-9669-4299 *Fax:* 612-9669-4144 • www.hayhouse.com.au

Published and distributed in the United Kingdom by: Hay House UK, Ltd., Astley House, 33 Notting Hill Gate, London W11 3JQ • *Phone:* 44-20-3675-2450 *Fax:* 44-20-3675-2451 • www.hayhouse.co.uk

Published and distributed in the Republic of South Africa by: Hay House SA (Pty), Ltd., P.O. Box 990, Witkoppen 2068 info@hayhouse.co.za • www.hayhouse.co.za

Published in India by: Hay House Publishers India, Muskaan Complex, Plot No. 3, B-2, Vasant Kunj, New Delhi 110 070 • *Phone:* 91-11-4176-1620 *Fax:* 91-11-4176-1630 • www.hayhouse.co.in

Distributed in Canada by: Raincoast Books, 2440 Viking Way, Richmond, B.C. V6V 1N2 • *Phone:* 1-800-663-5714 • *Fax:* 1-800-565-3770 • www.raincoast.com

~

<u>Take Your Soul on a Vacation</u>